Memories from the Blackdowns

The Blackdown
Writers' Group

Published in Association with

DEVON BOOKS

First published in Great Britain by Devon Books, 1999

We have been given such a wealth of material that we have not been able to fit everything into the text. Even if we have not mentioned your particular story or memory it will have been invaluable to us. It will have provided vital background knowledge, encouragement and colour, enabling us to complete this unique picture or Blackdown life.

ISBN 1 84114 025 2

Cataloguing in Publication Data

A CIP record for this title is available from the British Library

DEVON BOOKS
OFFICIAL PUBLISHER TO DEVON COUNTY COUNCIL

Halsgrove House
Lower Moor Way
Tiverton, Devon, EX16 6SS
United Kingdom
Tel: 01884 243242
Fax: 01884 243325
sales@halsgrove.com

Printed in Great Britain by WBC Ltd, Bridgend

THE BLACKDOWN WRITERS' GROUP

RESEARCHERS: Susan Doggett, Marian Bull, Olwen Gibson, Hazel Giles, Sue Lambert, Ann Smith.

ILLUSTRATOR: Eve Grosse.

COMPILER: Pamela Kellett.

TYPIST: Janice Lake.

We acknowledge, with gratitude, the grant given by the Millennium commission, through Help the Aged, that has enabled us to publish this book.

DEDICATION

This book is dedicated to Dr Jonathan E.D. Meads, in appreciation of his years of care for the people who live in these beautiful Blackdown Hills.

Foreword

MILLENNIUM PROJECT

These memories and stories come from the Blackdown Hills that straddle the Devon and Somerset border: a place of unspoilt valleys, hamlets and small villages with scattered farmsteads often hidden in the shadow of the hills. This book is not an historical document. We all remember things differently, so it records memories as seen through the eyes of those who experienced them, sad, happy, amusing, but above all fascinating.

Winters can be harsh, exposing the bare stony ground. In Spring and Summer the narrow twisting lanes are ablaze with wild flowers and the changing Autumn colours are breathtaking. Making a living from the land is always precarious and the old ways of life are changing. To add to those whose forebears have lived here for generations there is an influx of in-comers who are bringing new faces and fresh ideas into the hills. So, a new generation of Blackdown people is looking towards life in the new Millennium.

Perhaps, as you read these memories you will find you remember more. Whether they come from these Hills or from other areas of our beautiful countryside, pass them on so that our heritage will be saved for those who come after us.

Contents

"The Blackdown Hills are like the back of your hand, flat at the top and with your fingers spread out like the deep valleys where the rivers flow down to the sea."

"The Blackdown Hills called us to the heathers and the fuzz (ferns) and it was great as a small boy to have these lovely towering trees hiding one at play."

Introduction

A Childhood Memory

One of my earliest memories is being taken to Churchstanton Church and sitting with my family in the boxed pews - and not being able to see over the top of the wooden partition. There was no motor transport. We rode in our pony and trap, walked or bicycled along narrow, empty lanes. Rare visits were made to Taunton. We went in the pony and trap to Churchinford, and parked it in the stables behind the post office, before catching the bus. There was little need to shop. Everything was made at home. We grew most of our own food, had our own milk and eggs. What couldn't be provided was ordered from the grocer who called once a fortnight, and took the order for the next delivery.

I attended the Lady Sidmouth C. of E. School in Smeatharpe (now a private house). I walked to school, later bicycled, in all weathers. This was a happy place, never more than thirty children, even when the few evacuees came. At the front of the main classroom was a wooden panel. On Sundays this panel was opened to reveal an altar - and served as the Smeatharpe Parish Church. During the war all the school windows were latticed into diamond shapes with sticky tape to prevent the shattered glass falling on us.

Blackdown Experience

A warm May evening, just right for a walk down Threadneedle Street, The Cleeve and over the stiles to The Hams. I wander along the riverbank. A stillness as of complete peace and tranquillity overcomes me. I look at the hills where Culmstock Beacon stands sentinel over the valley, as the River Culm flows reassuringly on. What a beautiful place. I can hear the sound of silence. An occasional plop of trout, and a distant bird sings. The sun is slowly sinking towards the west enfolding everything in golden radiance. The sheep are golden smudges in the river meadows and the cows stand as plump golden statues. The river is a ribbon of molten gold; the grass under my feet is spattered with gold dust. The very air I breathe is gold. I am embraced by a warm, comforting presence which enfolds me. I surrender to this golden timelessness. Past, present and future merge as one. A feeling of complete happiness overcomes me. As the sun slowly disappears a final benediction, a flash of luminous blue as a kingfisher follows the course of the river to its rest. Heaven must surely be like this!

I walk slowly back across the fields with joy in my heart. The church, the cottages, the people lingering in their gardens all seem the same, but me, I am different. The experience has changed me. I will remember it forever.

Blackdown Traditions

The people from three of the Culm Valley villages were known to each other as Hemyock Herrings, Culmstock Baas, and Uffculme Ducks. This came about because of three well known stories circulating in the valley.

Hemyock Herrings

A Hemyock man had set his mole traps. Unbeknown to him some mates played a trick on him, they took the traps, sprung them on a herring and put them back in the ground. When the trapper inspected the traps next day he just could not understand how he had caught fish instead of moles.

Culmstock Baas

A story handed down in Culmstock is about the last man to be hanged for sheep stealing. The man lived in a cottage in the front garden to the left of Barley Cottage. He was called Tom Musgrave. One night in the local inn, his fellow drinkers were saying that the policeman had called on them looking for stolen sheep. Musgrave boasted that the policeman had not called on him, with the result that the next day the policeman heard of this and went to the cottage where he found the evidence. Tom Musgrave was tried at the Assizes in Exeter and hanged the next day at Heavitree. Over the years the story has also had various places for the hanging - Taunton, Waterloo Cross, Hillmoor, etc. but the story has always ended with the warning "Never say Baa to a Culmstock man."

Uffculme Ducks

A man kept Aylesbury ducks near Ashill. The ducks would paddle down stream foraging each day but would always return at night. One day the man had seen some Uffculme boys chasing the ducks and that night the ducks did not return. The village policeman was informed and he went to the local headmaster for help. "I'll find the culprits," he said. Next day he set the composition "What I had for Sunday Dinner". Beef, mutton, lamb, pork and the unsuspecting culprits wrote "Roast duck."

Nature's Harvests

Picking wild flowers and birds nesting were part of country life, and to find an oxslip or white bell was a real discovery. Cowslips were picked from the Roly Poly field at Whitebarn, when the game of Roly Poly was indulged in by we five children there. The field can still be seen when looking over the five-bar gate towards the Monument at Ford Street. The joy of the bluebells in the copse at Gortnell still brings back pleasant memories, and the perfume of a bunch of these flowers was really exciting. I had a collection of birds' eggs all those years ago, and, whilst it is banned nowadays, we were never destructive, taking one egg of a species only and blowing the contents out after pricking each end with a pin.

Seasons were pronounced: wortleberry, strawberry, nutting, mushrooming days were wonderful to look forward to. "Worts" were difficult to pick, so small - hundreds had to be picked for a tart, and hands stained by juice. Wild strawberries were small too, and at that time could be picked in the old chalk quarry between the "S" bend and Ford Street Hill.

Collecting mushrooms was a planned affair - five children walked across a field, spaced out in a straight line and no encroaching on each other's territory - I guess many a mushroom survived, left by one and missed by another.

Nutting was a Sunday treat, when Dad with his walking stick, having worked all day in the garden, was able to reach those nuts other arms could not reach.

Easter

On Good Friday morning, Mr Holloway would come to the door with a large basket of hot cross buns which we had then and there, hot for breakfast.

Hay Making

In those days it was hard living but much more fun than there is today. When it was hay time they would always go for a picnic in the hay field. First the hay was collected into rews (rows) of hay in the field. Then they used to gather it up into pooks or pucks. A favourite game was 'making sweet hay'. Young men and girls gathered in the hay field having fun pushing each other into the hay. One of the boys would pick up a piece of hay and twist it around into a long strand and then put it around a girl's neck and pull her towards him and then he would kiss her!

Cider Making

The cider orchard for Castle farm was in the field where Hemyock School and Parklands have now been built. They would collect the apples in September and October from the orchard by horse and cart and drive into the bottom yard. The apples were then bagged up and taken up the ancient wooden steps to the first floor apple loft. There was a hole in the floor and the apples were fed through the hole into the mill below to be chopped up. The mill was driven by an engine that at first stood outside and was connected to the mill by belts that passed through the slit window of the cellar and later by an engine that stood beside the mill.

❖

Mr Holway, the baker in Rosemary Lane, was famous for his double bakes. They were like Dorset knobs, cooked to a secret recipe and delivered in baker's dozens by pony and trap.

❖

❖

Mr. Nichols came as our new Rector to Clayhidon with his wife and family in a pony and trap. As they entered the parish (by Heazles) the pony was unhitched and a number of boys took the pony's place and pulled them to their new home.

❖

The chopped apples were then tipped into the press that stood in the cellar and formed into cheeses on the press. These were tipped into a frame and a horsehair blanket was put on top, then another layer was built up - about eight layers in all. The press was then screwed down onto the apples to squeeze out the juice. It would take two men to operate the press with long 8-9 foot poles. The juice was then collected in a wooden tub and poured into barrels. It would be kept for about three weeks in the barrels in order to let it 'work'. The rubbish would float to the top and the juice was racked - taken out and put into a clean barrel. The juice was then racked again for another three weeks.

The secret of making good cider lay in the racking. Racking had to be carried out at the right time. They would test to see if it was the right time by holding a lighted match above the barrel. If the gas given off by the fermenting juice blew out the match it meant that it was time for racking. The barrels were cleaned out in the stream. First the dregs were tipped out (being careful not to let the pigs eat the dregs or they would get drunk). They were rolled out between the Guard Houses down the bank into the water. Wooden staging was built along the stream for cleaning them.

Both the Prings and the Paynes used to sell cider locally and to pubs as far as Wellington. Every farm used to have an orchard to make their own cider from varieties such as Russets, Putts, Morgan Sweets, Jack Tuchers and Bell Apple. Sadly most of the Cider orchards are now gone.

It was the custom in this area for the poor children of the parish to go round from door to door on December 23rd and say - "Please we've come begging for Christmas". I would fill a basket with lovely large rosy apples usually Blenheim Oranges, and give them one each.

New Year

On Old Year's Eve we used to go to a Social in the Parish Hall. At midnight, as we came down Station Road, Dora's Granny Lowman would be standing by her open door to let the

New Year in and the back door to let the Old Year out. Each year we always looked for her to say 'Happy New Year.'

Ashen Faggots

One of my favourite memories was the burning of the Ashen Faggots. A few days before Christmas my two elder brothers would go to the woods where they cut green ash branches and made faggots by tying them with as many bonds as they could manage. On Christmas Eve, when all the yard work was finished and the cows were bedded down for the night, we all sat round the open hearth. The Ashen Faggot was brought in, in ceremonial fashion, then put on the fire to burn. Every time a bond was burned through we had a drink and a wish - cider for the elders and lemonade for the youngsters. We sang carols and old music hall songs and told ghostly stories until it was time to go to bed and hang up our stockings.

We were told that Father Christmas might be early and if he didn't find a stocking he wouldn't be able to fill it. So there was no pleading to stay up a little longer although sleep was always a long time coming. It came in the end and the excitement in the morning when we emptied our stockings was unforgettable.

It brings back so many memories when you start writing these things that I wonder what children of today will remember when they reach the senior citizen age.

Step Dancing

Step dancing was rather like tap dancing and it would be danced at parties such as at Ashen Faggot or Christmas. Both men and women would do it especially after the cider had flowed freely. Bob and Ern Parsons were well known step dancers. The music was usually a concertina.

❖

Churchstanton font was covered up and kept locked in the olden days as it was said to prevent witches from taking the holy water!

❖

One step dancing song went as follows:

Till you wink old woman,
Till you wink old man,
If you can't get a woman
Get an old can.

There were several verses to this song and they would become dirtier as the cider flowed, e.g. there was one verse with words 'Along came a lady with a fine pair of legs…'

Apart from step dancing there would be a concertina playing e.g. 'Farmer's Boy', 'She counted her money twice over' and ballads such as the one about a crippled boy stealing from his master the butcher to help his widowed mother and blind sister. The little boy worked for a butcher who did not pay him very much, His mother was widowed and his sister was blind. So to help his family one day the boy stole 5/- to take to his mother. Before his mother could take the money back, the butcher had discovered it was missing. The little boy was arrested and was in the dock:-

Mother

Policeman please remember
This is the first crime he's done
Remember I'm his mother
Pleading for her son.

Boy

Policeman do have pity,
So why should you be so unkind,
See my mother's left a widow,
Me a cripple and my little sister blind.

Children's Games

Children's games were marbles, hoops, whip tops, hop-scotch and skipping games. They skipped with a long rope in the playground, more children joining in as they chanted:-

My mother said that I never should
Play with the gypsies in the wood.
If I did, she would say
"Naughty little girl to disobey".

Queen, Queen Caroline
Washed her face in turpentine,
Turpentine made it shine
Then she used the mustard pot
Mustard pot made it hot
Queen, Queen Caroline

A ball was bounced against the wall to the chant "Plainsies, Clapsies, Round the World to Backsies, Touch your toe, Under you go, Plainsies, Clapsies."

During the long lamp-lit winter evenings, Snap, I-Spy, Snakes and Ladders, Shove Ha'penny and Ludo were played. Chestnuts were roasted and toast made on a wire toasting fork in front of an open fire.

Upottery Born and Bred

In 1916 two horsemen came into the Upottery village blowing bugles. They were recruiting men for the First World War and much later at the end of the war the church bells were rung on November 11th 1918.

Lord and Lady Sidmouth were quite an asset to Upottery as they owned a lot of property and employed many of the local people. They had shooting parties where they would take lunch out and bring back all the pheasants that had been shot. The keeper on the estate always collected his empty cartridges and would refill them. One of the keepers said he always carried a needle and cotton in case Lord Sidmouth ripped his clothes. One day he tore his trousers and the keeper sewed his shirt to his trousers but he never heard anything about it. A farmer though, shot a pheasant and was turned out of his farm! It was the Sidmouths' game and nobody dared shoot them!

The Sidmouths had a big chauffeur driven car, which was the only car in the village. When they had been away on duty for twelve months and their car arrived at the bottom of the hill everybody took turns with the ropes to tow them home. They employed a carter and cowman, several workers on the land, two carpenters, eight gardeners, footmen, batmen, several girls working in the house and a lady's maid for Lady Sidmouth. They would all come to church on Sunday.

The Sidmouths built Smeatharpe School and always took a great interest in its activities. One day every year they would give the school children an outing. Their carter would put some boards across the farm wagon, and take the children to Seaton for the day. All the wagons ran on iron wheels and I suppose the horse, when he got going, would do about five miles an hour.

There were fifty tenant farmers and twice a year they paid their rent. They always had a rent dinner for the farmers in the big room above the pub. I attended one of them and saw the farmers using a water siphon to blow the whisky out of their glasses. There was always a singsong and Sweet Molly Malone was sung every time.

Two Lord Sidmouths died in twelve months. The second developed pneumonia and died after he went to see to the water business at Wellsprings Farm. I suppose there must have been a bill to pay as Claridges of Exeter bought ten thousand trees off the estate. They had seven horses, which were kept at the pub, hauling the trees out for a long time. If they had a big tree they put the horses in a line, stood back and shouted one word and all the horses would pull their chains tight and move together, just like clockwork.

The Hemyock milk factory decided they would like to start a milk round in Upottery so they had a meeting at the Sidmouth Arms pub and said they would send a lorry round. They put a stand at Rawridge and in the pub yard at Upottery and came round with Vulcan lorries, which did 8 m.p.h. on solid tyres. We children ran and kept up with the lorry. The farmers took their milk in milk churns by horse and cart.

In the farmhouse where I lived there was a tailor. People would come from miles around to be measured for a suit of clothes, which he would make for them. A lady down in Rawridge did sewing and she would measure up to make the new outfits.

Langridges farm was let to my father Timon Bartlett and he farmed it for thirty-six years. They let me have the tenancy in 1936 and I started with £400 and they told me I was well off. I am still living there with sons and grandsons farming it now. I retired when I was 80, as I thought I had done enough!

I have been to Honiton market ever since I was three years old. Father and Mother would drive to Honiton on Saturday to the Black Lion pub and the ostler would tie up the horse. All the cattle would walk to market and if we took cows and calves to Honiton we'd have a little piece of holly

❖

A family had a mill down at Rawridge with a water wheel and all the machinery. It had been in the family for generations and people took their wheat there to have it ground, then took it home to make bread. A lot of people baked their own brown bread.

❖

to prick the calf to keep it going. There would be over 60 cows at the market and sometimes as many as 100.

The Culmstock Otter hounds came up through the River Otter to Upottery. Sometimes my father would drive his horse and trap to Royston water and go round Otterhead to meet them. Often we would see the otters swim in the water, they looked just like dishcloths moving about.
My wife and I went to the harvest festival at Clayhidon and the vicar up there told us "Any man can gather a good crop, but it takes a good man to gather a poor crop".

❖ ❖ ❖

On the way home farmers would stop at the Sidmouth arms and leave their horses tied up outside. On one occasion some boys changed all the reins around on the trap so when the farmer came out and pulled the reins the horse went the wrong way!

❖

Down on the Farm

Farming was the main occupation in the Culm valley until recently. Now many of the farms have been sold and divided up.

It was a leisurely morning's outing to take a cow to the bull. In Culmstock the only registered bull was at Dairy Court. After doing the morning's chores and having breakfast, the farmer would drive the cow at an unhurried pace through the village and turn it in with the bull. The men folk would then retire to the cellar to sample the cider and put the world to rights. If the cider was good I'm told the outing sometimes took all day!

Dairy Maid's Story

What could be better than getting up at 6a.m. on a lovely morning and going into the field with the grass all glistening with dew and the birds singing, to get the cows in for milking? The whole process of milking had to be done again in the early evening. It was usually the women who did the milking while the men worked in the fields.

Of course it was all hand milking in those days, sitting on a three-legged stool with a bucket between your knees, hoping that the cow would not kick you over, which happened sometimes. The milk was carried into the dairy and, if you were making butter, it had to be put through the separator which parted the cream from the milk. The cream was then put in a butter churn which was turned end over end to make it into butter, this was then sold. I remember a farmer man used to pack as much as he could on his bike and cycle to Taunton with it, wrapped up with dock leaves to keep it cool.

Young Farmers

In the early days, milk was taken to the milk factory in Hemyock by horse and trap. It was 1927 when the factory started to form a group of young farmers. Hemyock was the first place that started a club for farmers called the Hemyock Calf Club and I was one of the founder members. It is now known throughout many countries as the Young Farmers Club.

Horses also did all the work on the farm until the war, which brought tractors from the U.S.A. under Lease Lend arrangements. These were shared freely among neighbouring farmers.

A Culmstock Farmer

As a small boy growing up at Bartlett's farm, Woodgate, in the 1920's and 1930's, milking was part of my life right through until I retired.

We had about 12 cows and I was about 5 or 6 when I had my first attempt at milking. It looked easy, the squeeze, the pull and squish as the milk hit the bucket. It took me until I was 11 before I really mastered the knack. We would help get in the cows into the cobbled byre and on cold frosty mornings they would steam.

The milk would go into the dairy where it was put through the churn to make butter, then into the butter pats to squeeze out the water. Salt was added and it was made into ¹/₂lb pats of butter with a moulded picture on top. My mother took great pride in her butter making. Father had a motor bike and took the butter into a shop in North Street in Wellington.

The farmers took their milk in churns in their pony and traps to Dairy Court in the middle of Culmstock where it was collected and taken to Hemyock. Some of them only had a few cows and 2-3 gallons of milk, but it was a chance to meet other farmers and exchange news of farming and families. I remember one of our neighbours had to take the milk down himself when his farm worker was ill. Ponies are creatures of habit and the farmer was surprised when, on the way home, the pony turned into the back yard of a certain lady's house. He suddenly realised why it always seemed to take a long time when the worker took the milk!

In those days there would have been about a dozen people in the village of Culmstock who kept cows, sometimes only a house cow for their own use. Cows being driven slowly to and fro in the village was a common sight. Several of the farmers sold milk to villagers, people collected their milk in cans, often a task for the children. There were no rounds of bottled milk until the 1950's. In the late 1930's a family could make a living from about a dozen cows, a few sows, and 300-400 hens. The cows were fed on hay, turnips, swedes, mangolds, kale and a small amount of cattle cake. As soon as we were old enough my brother and I would take the pony and trap to fetch the cake on a Saturday. For bedding we would take the horse and cart up the White Path to the Beacon and cut ferns to fill up the shed.

We didn't grow a lot of corn, so we followed the reaper to chase rabbits. There were rats galore, sometimes so many in the rick you could almost see it moving. A neighbouring farmer would give us the runts from the litters of pigs and we would carry them home on our shoulders.

In 1933 the Milk Board was set up and there were new regulations, a lorry came from Wellington to collect our milk. It was one of the biggest changes to farming.

As we boys grew older I remember father sending to Yorkshire for some Shorthorn calves advertised in a farming magazine. They came on a passenger train tied up in a bag with just their heads sticking out. They never came to any harm but I'm sure it would not be allowed these days. We would rear a few of our own calves, perhaps from our favourite cows and sell the others. The newly hatched chicks would come in cardboard boxes by passenger train as well, The hens were all free range wandering across the fields but the foxes rarely took them. It was a boy's job to go round shutting up the fowl houses at night. We moved to Park Farm in 1940 and I farmed there until I retired. We had about 68 cows then. In my younger days life was hard but there was a

Life in the country was fun at times, and I loved the long summer days riding on the hay carts, collecting sacks of acorns for 1d for the pigs.

My grandfather used to take a firkin of cider, with his bread and cheese in a red handkerchief to the hay fields. He rarely reached home, but was found in a ditch over-inebriated, having quaffed too much of the amber liquid to quench his thirst.

certain contentment in the country way of life. The only control was the village copper, who knew everyone and everything and knew when to turn a blind eye.

Now everything is controlled and there are rules and regulations about everything.

My memories of Ford Street - the pigs at Mr. Down's farm at the bottom of our garden, squealing with fear, knowing their fate, and the scalding hot water to remove hairs from their skin.

Finding Water

Water is always to be found in the area but not always in the right spot! When I arrived here most of the farmers had a well. I did not, but I had plenty of spring water in the fields for the cattle. For farmhouse use the previous owners had dug a small depression in the ground so they could fill a bucket with a ladle then carry the bucket to the house and use it for washing, cooking etc. I decided to make the reservoir bigger and fitted a hand pump to a tap in the house. But it wasn't very good, so in the second year when I could afford it, I employed a builder to build me a well. This was successful but still not enough water.

At the bottom of the farm there was a lot of water so I linked up the springs and connected them to a big brick container about a quarter mile from the farmhouse and fitted a 2″ pipe from the container to a 'Ram'. This ram I got from the agricultural merchants in Wellington. They wanted to sell me a new one but I couldn't afford it so I said "What about a second hand one?". He said "You can have this for £8 but it doesn't work". I bought it and being a qualified engineer I took it home and fitted two taps to it and it worked beautifully. I connected it up to the dairy and I had water any time I wanted it!

Tipsy Sow

Every year we made a lot of cider from the apples in our orchard and there were 6-10 hogsheads lined up on the jibs in the cellar, for the year's consumption. Any visitor, delivery man, thatcher whoever, always had to be offered a drink. The glasses were kept on top of the barrels for anyone to help themselves, if we were out in the fields.

One day we arrived home to find the old sow tottering about the yard, drunk as a lord. The cellar door had not been properly closed and she had gone in, nosed around the tap and knocked it out and supped to her heart's delight.

Up to the time the war started we had a market behind the now Catherine Wheel, and some of the animals sold were driven down Station Road to be put on our local train, along with tanks of milk from our factory.

I was brought up on a farm at Leigh and lived there until I retired. As a boy I rode my pony to Culmstock school in the 1930's and left it at the Railway Inn with the landlord, Mark Bowman. I was one of five and the only one to go to Culmstock School, I don't really know why, maybe it was because my father thought Mr. Bull would keep me in order. I never did get the cane, though I got pretty near it!

I always loved horses and, of course, all the work on the farm was with horses when I was a boy. By the time I was twelve I was ploughing with horses and up at 6a.m. to help milk the cows before I went to school, and milked again in the evening when I got home. In the summer we would milk out in the fields.

At hay making time everybody, family, friends and neighbours would help. The hay was loose and loaded on the wagons with pitchforks with somebody up top making the load, keeping the corners up in a good even load and tying down with rope to take it to the rick. At the end of the day everyone sat down to a ham supper with plenty of cider. We didn't grow corn until the war when we were compelled to grow some. Mr. Alec Blackmore and a Mr. Chapman came round to tell you what to grow and who would be exempt from joining up. At harvest time the corn was cut round and round the field, and when it was near the centre the rabbits would make a run for it and the men would be ready with guns and dogs to catch them. When the traction engine came for threshing, once again everyone would help.

After the war in the 50's I rode point-to-point and I kept five racers. I still have all the cups I won. I raced all the time and loved it. Apart from horses, the pub, beer and skittles was my entertainment.

Mr. Hine at Hidon Mill used to grind the grain. The children went to him to get a peck of grain for their hens, which he measured out very slowly with finger and thumb. His daughter, Mrs. Northover, had a round hut at the Mill, from which she sold sweets and tobacco. Children were allowed to look for eggs and were paid if they found any.

❖

We killed our own pigs, salted the pork and also killed our own lambs and bullocks, then shared it around with other people and they would do the same.

❖

An Old Farmer's Memories

When I was only young we came down from London during the First World War, and I am 94 now. My sister used to help on the farm, and her duties were to look after the meadow and glean on the hill. My father had some steers he wanted to fatten up for the butcher's shop so one day he took out two of the milking cows and replaced them with the steers. Well, when milking time came my sister started up one end of the pen and I started down the other end. There was a commotion and I heard my sister giggle. Course I realised what it was, no one had mentioned a word to her about replacing the cows, and she sat down in the dark and tried to milk the steers! That was a joke that took her a long time to live down.

We had a contract with Wides eggs to go up to London several times a week. We had to take all the eggs to London, Sainsbury's taking 150, and sometimes we brought 150 boxes back.

We were driving all night, because we used to leave Uffculme in the evening and get to Blackfriars early in the morning. There were no lights then, only those baffle plate army lights, and the light only shone about a few yards in front of your vehicle, but we knew the roads blindfolded nearly.

Land Girl

Having done one month's training as a land Girl at Whiteways, Whimple, I was posted to Garlandhayes, a farm at Clayhidon on the Blackdown Hills. It was a mixed farm of 100 acres run by the farmer, his wife and an experienced worker. There was a baby daughter and a bedridden Granny (she loved me to tell her all the gossip). There were cows, sheep, pigs, poultry and two horses, sheep dog and cats.

The farmer grew wheat, oats, barley and pasture. We had a tractor, carts, cutter and binder, rake, ploughs and harrow. The farmhouse had two living rooms, four bedrooms, bath H & C. The kitchen had an Aga and a sink with a hand pump from a well for drinking. At the back was a dairy and pantry, also a wash house with a copper and dolly tub. Outside the house was a large barn, stables and cowsheds. Until we had a generator for electricity we put up with oil lamps and a Tilley and an oil stove before the Aga. We also had a TELEPHONE!

I arrived during the winter so was very glad of a warm welcome and a feather bed which made it difficult to get up at 6a.m. After a cup of tea and a double bake, I took a lantern, to start hand milking. Two hours later I came in for breakfast of eggs with bacon from the home-killed pig. The sheds were cleaned out and the dung put in the middle of the yard and then brushed and hosed. The worst job in the winter was cutting kale in the freezing rain and snow but in wet weather I worked in the barn grinding corn and picking over potatoes. Another hard job was loading a cart with dung and driving the horse up to a field to spread the dung with a fork. When necessary I took Captain to a local forge to be shod. I was given 6d for a drink while I waited. The free range poultry were checked every night because of foxes and badgers and the sheds had to be cleaned and creosoted regularly.

In the spring, besides the general routine of ploughing and sowing, I went horse hoeing, picking up and carrying buckets of stones to the edge of the fields. I had to cut the patches of thistles with a goad. During the early summer I helped to shear the sheep by turning the handle of the mechanical shearer. Sometime in June we would be haymaking using the horse to cut the hay which we then turned with hand rakes. When it was dry it was loaded and built into a rick.

It was then time to have my one week's holiday before the harvest. When the corn was ripe it was cut and tied into sheaves which we stacked to dry until threshing time.

All the neighbours around came to help with the threshing. The machine was hired and came on a set date. It caused a lot of clatter and dust. The sacks weighed two and a half hundredweight and I stood in the lorry moving them to the back. There was not much time for a social life but I enjoyed going once a week to see my friend Dorothy (Culverwell) and her family. There was W.I., darts and skittles at the Merry Harriers and we would cycle to the bus stop to go to Taunton.

Sometimes the bus refused to go up the hill coming home, so the passengers had to get out and push! Dances were occasionally held in the room above the Half Moon, well attended by the G.I.'s from Dunkeswell and Smeatharpe. One dark night a particularly frisky one was difficult to get rid of so I led him to a field full of sheep and escaped while he blundered among them.

The only other Land Girls I met were the rat catchers from Exeter.

Hemyock 45 years ago

When I came to live in Hemyock in the early 1950s it was a remote agricultural village. Being a farmer, I was used to the farming aspect but it was the remoteness that struck me. The village was only eleven miles from the bustling county town of Taunton but the Blackdown Hills were very much a secret, unexplored part of England.

People still relied on horse transport or feet! The steep escarpment up from the Somerset side and the even steeper drop into Hemyock were a considerable deterrent. So, people found it easier to drift gently down the valley to Cullompton and Tiverton. The railway also drew people to stay in Devon as it wove its tortuous way down from its terminus in Hemyock to Tivvy Junction, as Tiverton Junction was affectionately known.

Few people in the village had cars, only the doctor, rector, garage owners and some small business men such as builders and shopkeepers and a few farmers. The newly acquired tractor was the means of transport into the village with the farmer's wife riding up behind. Many a farm and cottage outside the village had no mains water or electricity. In the village the sewage was discharged neat into the Culm!!

This isolation meant that the village had always generated its own entertainment with a large number of clubs and societies meeting in the Parish Hall. Originally this incorporated a cinema projection room, now expanded into the upper floor of the store room.

The economy of the parish was geared to farming. Hemyock livestock market, behind the Catherine Wheel, closed at Christmas 1954. Until then, driven cattle and sheep would have been part of the scene in the village, and woe betide anyone whose front gate was not hastily closed. The largest employer was the milk factory, about 80 people, mostly living in the parish. It was then a farmers' dairy, taking milk from some 350 farms all over the Blackdowns. The herds ranged in size from 10 cows up to 30, with very few in excess of 40. Milk lorries clanked through the village from 7a.m. to 3.30p.m. every day, but no one complained as it was Hemyock's life blood. The milk left Hemyock on the afternoon train for London's Wood Street dairy. During the day the empty rail tankers were winched one by one across the road into the factory and fell back under gravity into the station yard. There were two egg packing stations employing mostly women, and egg collection lorries visited the farms twice weekly. The driver brought with him a sealed packet of cash for last week's eggs. No robberies or muggings in those days.

The ironmonger stocked all farm requisites from wellington boots to automatic drinking bowls and George Small (Devon) Ltd of Uffculme kept a store and yard above the station supplying feedstuffs, fertilisers and bags of coal. Blacksmiths/Farriers were to be found in the village square and at Whitehall.

Conditions in the home were hard and the work was heavy. The weekly wash meant lighting the copper and using a scrubbing board. The fortunate few possessed a mangle, but for most it was hand wringing and then out on the clothes line. Cooking was done on a coke-fired range, no wall-to-wall carpet, just linoleum in the front parlour with perhaps a small rug. The rest of the house had to be scrubbed with a scrubbing brush on hands and knees. The W.C., if there was one, was accessible either from outside the house or it meant a trip down the back garden path to the shed at the bottom. There might be a soak away which was always in danger of polluting the well. No wonder 20 years later OAPs in the village, looking back to their parents' retirement, couldn't believe their luck.

A Farmer's Wife

I was a city child, born and bred in Manchester and my school days were filled with the war years and my teens spent training to become a secretary. Who would have thought that I would end up as a farmer's wife? Quite a change from being a secretary to a linguist who had a translation bureau above the Swiss Consulate in Manchester Piccadilly!

In 1942 when I started work we had a bad epidemic of foot and mouth disease so I had to walk through a trough of disinfectant. The cattle right up the valley were slaughtered on the farms and buried in lime in the fields. Every farm had great mounds of soil in the fields where the cattle had been buried.

I joined the Land Army for the last twelve months that it existed. Thus began my enduring love of cows, the country side and farming folk. After some five years working at an animal sanctuary and then working with pedigree cattle, I married a farmer and began a real partnership in every sense of the word.

We came to the Blackdowns in 1966 to take on the tenancy of Burnworthy Farm. We brought with us, from Dorset, our herd of pedigree Friesian cattle and followers. John was born in Dorset and farmed with his father on the gentle, fertile and free draining soil. At 800 to 900 feet the harsh, stony, wet land on the Blackdown Hills came as a culture shock to us and probably even more so to our cattle. We were dismayed to find our older cows became arthritic from the wet lying land. The herd developed local diseases like tick-borne fever, died with blackleg, nibbled rhododendrons and were poisoned. All this was new to us and we had to learn fast how to adapt. The stress was offset by the sheer beauty of the Blackdown Hills and the wonderful friendship of the people who lived and farmed on them. Neighbours gave us advice and labour, as and when we needed it. With the farm, we inherited a workman who had been at Burnworthy, man and boy and knew every stick and stone on the place. His name was Bert Taylor, he lived at Clayhidon and came to work on his motor bike or, if the weather was really bad, he walked. Always on time and never a grumble. An excellent worker and a natural gentleman, he was a bachelor and lived alone. Every year, on his birthday, we had a skittles party and supper at the Half Moon Inn. All his friends and neighbouring farmers came. We have wonderful memories of his old friend Jimmy singing country songs, a favourite one being 'And I never said naught about ought'. How we wish that we could have recorded him.

Our day began at 5a.m., seven days a week. The milk lorry from Hemyock arrived at 7.20 each morning and our milk churns had to be labelled and ready for the driver. On Christmas day the lorry came one hour earlier, so it was 4 a.m. start for us. Hard work, long hours, but happy days full of real job satisfaction.

How things have changed. In the sixties and seventies, within a mile radius of Burnworthy, we had at least 16 dairy farms. Now only one, probably the smallest, remains. Land sold off, farm houses developed into luxury homes, sheep instead of cattle, young people drifting away, village shops struggling. We wonder what the future holds for our beloved Blackdowns.

Rabbits

I was working at Wides in the late 1940's. The rabbits would come in hampers from the farms. They would be double hocked so that they could carry them over a stick when they were out rabbiting. Bert Hill and I would unhock them, sort the shot from the trapped, grade them and weigh them, and then hock them again. We would be surrounded by rabbits. When we'd re-packed them again in the hampers, we would take them down to Hemyock Station to go to Smithfield and other places. The farmers got about sixpence each for them.

I was still living at home when my mother asked me to go out one night and shoot a rabbit for the pot. It was getting dusky and there didn't seem to be any rabbits about. Usually I'd creep round a corner and would see one. Down across the field I thought I could see one move so I shot it, but when I walked across the field I found I'd shot a dung heap! When I got home and Mother asked me if I'd got one I said I didn't think she'd want what I'd shot that night.

Father was 'in tea' in India but came home before the First World War because Mother was ill. He rented Culm Davy House from the Folletts in 1913 and bought it in 1921 with some land from the Follett estate. He was the first man in the valley to have a tractor. Frank Lowman, who had been gassed in the war, was the cowman and lived further up the hill in Culm Davy. My father had forty shorthorns for milk, all of which had Biblical names such as Hepzibah. The unpasteurised milk produced on the farm was made into butter and sent up to London on the train to a restaurant in Bond Street. He kept Wyandotte hens but unfortunately one day Hepzibah, who was adventurous, ripped the wire from around the hens and they scattered everywhere!

The family sold the farm when my father died in 1969 and most of the land was sold separately.

Art worked for farmers in the area before going to the milk factory. Among other things, he milked the cows at Highwood Farm for Mr Cole for 11/- a fortnight. They used a three legged stool, a lantern and a bucket. Often, by the time they got to the dairy, the lantern had blown out so it was just candles.

It was easier to take a tin bath full of clothes to the stream and leave them in the stream for the clothes to soak than to carry the water back to the house for washing. The clothes were carried back to be put through the mangle. Later when myxomatosis was prevalent the water had to be pumped up the hill and it was then piped into the house direct. Electricity was brought into the cottage in 1948 and was connected by Mr Cox for £19.

Old Farmhouses
Callers Farm, Rosemary Lane

I moved with my family into Callers Farm in March 1907. The house is in two different parts - the 'new' part and the old. As a child growing up there, it was the old part that fascinated me.

Upstairs, one stepped from a dark little room where we stored the harvest apples, down into a long narrow bedroom. Its little window at one end was almost floor level, but

❖
When Art and Betty were married in 1948 they lived in Chapel Cottage at Culm Davy with water available from a pipe a field away. It took three quarters of an hour to fill a bucket!
❖

not quite, for there was a low window seat. The door leading into this room had a round hole in it, and a large wooden latch just above the hole. On entering one pushed one's finger through the hole and lifted the latch. Possibly once there was a bobbin so that it was a case of "pulling the bobbin, lifting the latch and walking in" - just like Red Riding Hood!

Opposite the door was another with two panes in the top half. On opening it, one found oneself in a gallery or loft, part way over the kitchen. Rather terrifying for the very young. On the left and down below was the kitchen with its stone floor and only a narrow partition about 18 inches high between us and the stone floor below.

The ceiling rose to quite a height over that part of the kitchen that was not under the loft. To reach the cobwebs one would stand on a chair, on the table, wielding a long-handled broom! There were those who thought the old part of the house to be Saxon. Could the loft once have been a minstrel's gallery? The chimney corner in the kitchen and under the 'gallery' was very cosy one side, but sooty rain could come down the other, with a glimpse of the sky as one looked up. On the cosy side an iron door opened into a large brick cavity - the bread oven - no longer used as such. We stored our home made jam in it. Across the chimney place was an iron bar from which hung a kettle, boiler and baking crock. Home cured hams from home-reared pigs were also suspended from large nails driven into the chimney walls.

On one side of the kitchen, directly underneath the afore-mentioned old bedroom, was the dairy with a window at each end,

and curiously, a trap door in the ceiling opening into the old bedroom. The dairy housed the separator, butter churn and butter roller. Later, after we had left the farm, an interesting discovery was made - an ancient arched doorway in the dairy wall. It led into a cupboard which opened through a doorway into one of the rooms in the 'new' part. We used to keep our books on shelves in that cupboard. The 'new' part is probably about 200 years old with ancient fireplaces, and old beamed ceilings.

Culm Davy House

This was originally thatched and thought to have been an old Priory but burned down in 1890 when a parlour maid had trouble lighting a fire. One day it would not go so she poured paraffin on to it and everything caught fire! A stone farmhouse was built on the foundations in 1900. During their time there my family had a succession of twenty-three parlour maids, including Cissie Lowman. They were trained to run the house and cook until they left to get married when they were given a present of a Singer sewing machine. They were also given feathers from the Wyandotte hens which were sterilised in the Aga to make eider downs.

Crocker's Farm

When I was first married I went to live at Crocker's farm, where the kitchen was really primitive. The walls were painted with lime white wash every spring. The water pump was outside, and it took a hundred strokes of the pump to get the water flowing! After milking, the milk needed to be cooled, which took a lot of pumping! The kitchen had a stone floor and an open fireplace with firedogs and brandise (a trivet) and crooks for the kettle and boiling pot. Every day I had to chop and saw a wheelbarrow full of wood to keep the fire going. Later oil was used and then a Rayburn was installed. There was no sink in the kitchen so the washing up bowl was kept on the table. Crocker's farmhouse used to house servants, with the servants' bell connected to the main part of the house. Long after the servants had left the house, the bell could still be heard ringing. On investigation it was found that rats walked along the bell wires, making them ring.

Smeatharpe Bride

In 1950 we arrived in 'Smeathearpe' (that additional 'e' appeared on the signpost and map in the late '50s) in true hillbilly style, teetering in an open builder's lorry. It was a bleak day in early January as we moved into a patchily thatched old cottage which had been empty for a year, without a single facility and we had a four month old baby. We found his cot blanket covered with a dew of moisture next morning. However the kindliness of the neighbours evidenced itself from the first day as a tray of tea and treasured fruit cake, a great treat in times of rationing, welcomed us as we settled our belongings.

Cottages for sale were rare at that time, most of them being rented, and this being the furthest afield in the Sidmouth estate, we had to buy two houses to acquire one, and sell off the second. With a primus stove running all day, our immediate task was the installation of the first Rayburn in the village, with a rotary pump supplying a storage tank from the well outdoors, fifteen hundred pump strokes to fill the tank.

At this time few houses had much more than water, some form of cooking heat and an open fire. Clothes were boiled in a 'copper' with fire underneath, baths were zinc, toilets graduated from earth closets to

chemical, the latter even in the village hall where dances, children's parties and sales took place.

Smeatharpe then was really self-sufficient, having its own historic Baptist Church, forge, sawmills, run by steam engine, an early Fordson tractor, a pub, builders, milk supplier, post office and a highly commended school with a little Church of England sanctuary, which during the week was screened off with panelling now to be seen in Upottery Church. Many scholars served and too many died in the two world wars, their memorial board now in the Hall.

Everybody took their gardening very seriously, the men vying with one another in the allotments, enjoying a jar of home made cider afterwards. Local fruits made potent wine or mead brewed by several beekeepers, with gifts of honey popular.

Almost all the shopping could be done through salesmen at the door, two grocers, two bakers, three butchers, fishman, clothes van, paraffin and hardware and the chemist. The car being used by the bread winner, family needs were thus supplied, with perhaps a town visit on market day. The van system came to an end with the increase in petrol prices.

The school teachers were of a very high standard, in early days taking children through their school lives, and later from five to eleven, many then winning scholarships. Teachers also dried out sodden children's clothes as they walked a long way to school in all weathers, perhaps from over the airfield. They arranged quite a social calendar of sports, harvests, plays and carol services. After the closure of the school the village social life, as bound up with the children, never fully recovered. The closure was reported widely locally and in the London papers in 1958, being hotly disputed by the three M.Ps representing Smeatharpe, a border village between two constituencies, also with Lady Sidmouth taking the argument with petition to the floor of the House of Commons.

In 1952 a few local mothers decided to found a W.I. which has been enthusiastically supported since, with members from surrounding villages, resulting in an atmosphere quite its own.

A good deal of building has doubled the housing to around 40. Across nearly 50 years daily life, times and expectations have changed, with much being updated, but through joys and sorrows, busy life in Smeatharpe has much to commend it. Any young readers please note, we have never suffered from boredom.

The Butcher, The Baker, The Candlestick Maker...

A variety of memories of the shops and businesses within the Blackdowns and the characters who ran them.

Memories of Rosemary Lane

Once, long ago, when children could wander along country roads and explore fields and woods without fear, Rosemary Lane was a very different place from what it is now.

Mrs. Gill would sit at the window of Hope Cottage (Oak Cottage now) with her sewing machine, for she was the village dressmaker. Her window opened onto the road and often friendly folk would stop for a chat with her over the window sill. On the opposite side of the road was the well from which she drew water - such cold, clear water. Just above the cottage was the creeper covered chapel, and opposite was the blacksmith's forge, where my father used to take his horses to be shod. No tractors in those days.

The next building in the lane was Rosemary Cottage. Over the door of the porch was the sign DEVON CONSTABULARY. The policeman lived there with his wife and child. Sometimes he came to the afternoon service at the Chapel on Sundays and when he was there, I felt I must be good and not turn round or fidget as that was being naughty.

The tiny cottage behind the Constabulary was inhabited by a dear old lady called Miss Rawling. We children used to post her letters to save her going up the very steep bit of hill. The Post Office (now South View) was run by a Miss Nix and her father. We loved the blue-eyed, white-haired

old man because he was always kind and used to give us sweeties - sweets were rare in those days. There was a cottage with a stable and trap-house attached and the two places were used by Mr. Holway, the baker, for his horses and covered baker's van. Everyday he and his assistant would go out after the baking, delivering the bread.

Churchinford

Originally, the Churchinford Post Office had Georgian gothic style windows and was fitted all around with attractive shelves with turned supports and a bulls-eye window looking into the sitting room - the kind of setting for a Jane Austen film. Only stationery and the occasional box of bloaters was sold there, and in 1923 my father brought home some tea and a pound of tobacco, much to the annoyance of the shopkeeper across the road. In the late 1920's my father drove his chain driven Durrant van, under contract to the G.P.O., between Churchinford and Chard. This was when we were in the Chard postal area. During the General Strike he had an armed escort to ensure that the mail got through.

My mother moved into the Post Office on her marriage in 1931. She always said that shopping was fun in those days. Butter, cheese and lard came in big blocks and had to be cut up and weighed. They sold practically everything - boots, bicycles, hardware, batteries, haberdashery, clothes. Men would come in and say "Ralph (my father's name) I want a working shirt, or I want a best shirt!" My grandfather would drive to Taunton to collect ice as they made their own ice cream.

A man used to come up from Taunton Telephone Office to encourage people to have the phone installed. If there were nine subscribers, Churchstanton could have its own exchange. He would hire a bicycle for a few pence a day from my parents and they would suggest whom he should visit and the poor man would cycle all over the parish to drum up some interest. How different from today when most homes have at least one phone!

Hemyock

Hemyock had Wides Egg and Poultry establishment, the saw yard, the cemetery, the butter factory, a baker's shop where the Mace shop is today, and the school on the corner. The Post Office was a shop owned by Mrs Wilcox who sold sweets. She was also an agent for a Wellington Jeweller so one window of the shop was full of jewellery, brooches and necklaces which were lovely to look at. A shop stood where Egypt car park is now, the owner had a pony and trap and bought rabbit skins and his wife sold sweets. At Easter the children put their hands through the gate of the shop, and the lady would put little packets of sweets in them, then the children changed hands and hoped the lady would put another packet in the other hand. The lady's name was Mrs Hine, she had grey hair, and corkscrew curls hanging down the side of her face.

Up the High Street was another baker, a shop selling groceries and two pubs next to one another but the Star burnt down. At the bottom of Castle Hill, Mr. Hall was the cobbler, and next door his son Frank had a butcher's shop.

Dad gave me three pence on Mondays, 2½d was for milk and ½d I could have for sweets. We used to go up to Amos White's shop and buy a ha'peth of the biggest sweets we could find so that we had a good weight. We used to say "Famous Amos, the grocery man, he tries to diddle us if he can". Mrs Bird had a sweet shop which is now the hairdressers. Mr. Yeandle came each week to cut hair.

The Monday cattle market was held behind the pub. The bakery run by Mr. and Mrs John Stradling was opposite the old school, a large loaf of bread was 4d. Mr. Bill Hall had the shop, now Spar. He did some repairs and sold laces and studs for football boots. He was so untidy that when my father went up to collect a pair of shoes he could only find one and brought the other one down a day or two later. Redwoods bus started in 1932 and did a wonderful service for the village. A stream ran down along the side of High Street. People used to dip water from there,

In the High Street Carricks sold everything. Hobnail boots hung down from the ceiling, and they hung there until they were rusty. Behind the counter was a window through to the living room with a shelf and bottles of sweets on it.

so we called it Shutlake! Along Broadway there was a blacksmith's shop owned by Mr. Paul, and Charlie Chubb used to work for him. We often watched him shoeing horses, we could just reach to look over the half door. Mr. Turner had everything from boots, shoes, slippers, wool, haberdashery, groceries and sweets. I can remember my dad taking me to the shop Up Steps to buy some shoes but unfortunately he spotted a pair of black high laced boots, just right for the winter, but I hated them. Just think, they are in fashion now.

Early Days at Doble's Garage

Doble's Garage in Station Road, Hemyock started life in a small building and £50 in the owner's pocket. With bicycles, motorcycles, radios, and batteries, and doing a lot of repair work on cars and tractors it was hard work. During the war there were Americans stationed in the area and they became regular visitors when they found bicycles for sale. On one occasion one of them was stopped by the local policeman who accused him of riding without a rear light, to which the American replied "It's all right, the front light is enough to see where I am going".

Mr. Doble eventually built a new and larger garage on the other side of the road and moved there in 1946. There were a few problems to overcome when the first petrol tank was fixed, as the pit kept filling up with water. They had difficulty in making the tank stay down. When another tank was fitted later it was chained in place. The lorry bringing the cement tipped it out at one end and the weight of it tipped the tank. The cement set and the tank was permanently fixed at an angle. During the war Mr. Doble realized there was a market for second hand cars and he went to London hoping to find a contact in one of the large garages there. Sure enough he did, and for years he made trips to and from London to bring cars back to the West Country. Many a time he would catch a train late in the afternoon to pick up a car and drive it back. This was not easy as there were precious few lights on the way and of course, no signposts. More than once he was stopped and questioned. In one instance he was hauled off to a police station to give an account of himself! Not much fun in the middle of the night.

Life at home was not all plain sailing either. One good customer kept complaining about a rattle in her car. The mechanic tried this and that but still the rattle continued, until someone discovered a Corona bottle beneath the engine!!

During all these war years, apart from being in the forces, Mr. Norman Lowman was a wonderful helpmate. He started at fourteen and stayed until the business was sold in 1976.

John Stradling kept a bakery where the Post Office is now and the two houses adjoining were all thatched, you could buy a large packet of broken Smith's crisps for 1d. The next house up from the bakery was called Egypt House where our local Nurse called Bray and her parents kept a fruit shop where we could buy a lovely rosy apple for 1d. Across the road was Mrs. Bird's shop, where you could get a tube of sherbet for ½d.

There was a shop called Up Steps owned by Miss Hyde and she kept just everything, even having old Mr. Bill Turner who made suits of clothes. The Post Office, complete with telephone switchboard, was kept by Mrs. Morgan and her mother Mrs. Hine who had a huge grandfather clock that stood in the corner. Old Mr. George Morgan used to deliver newspapers on his bike. Down Station Road Alfred Cox's mother and her sister Miss Parish kept the laundry shop and also sold crockery. Further down the road my father, Frank Salter, had a carpenter, undertaker and wheelwright shop, and Reg James had a grocery shop with slot machine where a packet of cigarettes cost 2d for 5! Next door Henry Smith kept one butcher's shop and another was kept by Bill Drake, opposite the church. The present Spar shop was Bill Halls cobbler's shop where boots and shoes were mended. At the bottom of Station Road was an Italian hairdresser called Dellcarter.

The Halifax agents used to be a sweet shop run by Mrs. Jenny Webber and husband Harold. At Hemyock Motors, Alfred Cox kept a bicycle shop, later Donald Clare ran it, and at the bottom of High Street was the late Dr. Huth's surgery.

Hemyock Bakery and Post Office

We found out about a bakery from Mr. Hart and moved to Hemyock in January 1947. The bakery hadn't been used for 35 years so we were virtually starting from scratch. At first we moved to the Gables in Station Road because the bakery was such a mess and we had a lot of work to do. It was overrun with rats and mice because it was previously an old saddler's business. There was an old side flu oven heated with coal and coke. The fire was made in the side and then pulled out when it was hot enough. It was then washed out before we could bake the bread. Quite a job, believe me, but we managed it.

On the first day we burnt all the bread which was very sad. But I went round the village with two little children, and a baby of six months in my arms and told everybody we'd burnt all the bread but if they didn't buy it we couldn't make any more because we couldn't afford to buy any more flour. We sold every loaf! The village accepted us well - we were Devonshire people which makes a difference in a place like this.

We delivered the bread in a little brown van, which was fairly reliable and went as far as Luppitt, Dunkeswell and other villages. We had the van repaired at Wide's garage, round the corner by the egg packing station. A lot of people came into the shop to buy pop, crisps, cakes, as well as bread but we couldn't afford any other stock.

We would be up early in the morning and working very late at night so our days were very long. My husband had worked in an old bakery in Kentisbeare where it was the custom to cook the Christmas turkeys every year so we thought it would be the right thing to do here. Anybody could bring a turkey down and we would charge them 2/6 to cook it. One old lady turned up with her turkey on Christmas Eve when we were very tired. It hadn't been drawn or stuffed. I said "We can't take it like that, you have to draw and stuff it first" So she said "What the hell are we paying 2/6 for?"

At Easter we made hot cross buns. I stayed up to sort the shop out the night before, then my husband would get up at 1a.m. to get the bread going. We baked the bread first, then the buns and delivered them in a cart round the village. The buns were always hot, people complained if they weren't hot! But we used to manage.

Then we moved to where the Post Office is now on March 17th 1951 where we rented the premises as we could not afford to buy it. Of course, later we bought the premises. We had stock to buy, that took all our money. We were able to bake bread straight

away as the ovens had been looked after well. Although the oven was such a big improvement, it was still an old side flu oven but 'moderner'. It was called a steam tube oven and was very good. My husband liked it a lot better but it was still hard work with lots of shovelling. We used to complain, until we changed to an oil fired one.

In the winter of 1963 the weather was very bad. It went on so long, about three months. Because we had such a demand my husband was baking round the clock. Although some people had dealt outside the village before, they were so glad of us then. The farmers used to come down to the milk factory with the milk, then they would pack the bread in the churns and take it back with them. It was a job to get oil and flour of course as the oil came from Bridgwater. We were very worried about it but we got it eventually. My husband rang them about it and told them how difficult it was and what a demand he had. So they said "We will get through to you on one condition and that is, can we have 6 loaves when we come back". So that is what it cost us extra!

There were a lot of shops in Uffculme - and several places of worship, all well attended, with children in best clothes, girls with hats and gloves. Polly Willand from the sweet shop and Mrs Long from the general shop appeared in church in feather bonnets.

Travelling salesmen visited our home. Mr. Sing came on a bicycle with clothes for sale in a basket. Mr. Billson came up from Honiton in a van and sold many things. I remember buying a skirt from his van. There was a Tap shoe (cobbler).

I had worked in the Post Office for years since I was at school, in Exeter and Cullompton, so in 1965, when Mary Morgan was giving up the Post Office, we took it over. We continued till 1984, when my husband died. I kept the business going because my daughter could do the baking and I had help of good local staff who were like a family to me. Then after three years I decided to retire.

Culmstock Post Office

Mr. and Mrs. George Taverner took over the Culmstock Post Office in 1924 and ran it until their retirement in the early 1950's. It meant long hours and hard work. The mail would arrive soon after 6a.m. and they would both sort the letters to be delivered by bike around the parish by Mr. Taverner and Albert Pike of Myrtle Cottage, Hillmoor. Then Mr. Taverner would return home for breakfast having worked up an appetite. Meanwhile, the daily papers would have arrived by the first train up from Tiverton Junction and our Post Master would go down and sort them into rounds for delivery in the station waiting room. There would be an afternoon delivery of mail, all by bicycle! Douggie Forward was always taken on to help at Christmas, but in those days the Christmas rush only lasted about a week and there was always a delivery on Christmas Day.

Mrs. Taverner looked after the Post Office, Nita Slowman worked there for some time and after that Daisy Channon. Lloyds Bank opened for business in the sitting room on Mondays and customers waited in the hall with the door discreetly closed so as to preserve the customer's confidentiality. Telegrams were delivered and, in those days before telephones were widely used, they often brought bad news. Mrs. Taverner wrote them out by hand and several people still cherish Wedding Day telegrams in her fine handwriting. When Uffculme Post Office was closed for their half day on Thursdays Mr. Taverner had to deliver the telegrams to Uffculme Parish as well. One of the most upsetting jobs was to deliver telegrams informing that a son was killed or missing in the war.

A Village Maid

Betty was the youngest of nine children, seven girls and two boys. The family originally came from near Kentisbeare where her father was a farm labourer. In those very early days she went with a pram to fetch coal, paraffin and accumulator batteries for the radio from Kentisbeare. About 1940, when she was nine, they moved to the cottage in Madford, where she still lives, on a small holding with six or seven cows. When they first went to live in the cottage there was no electricity so they were dependent on oil lamps and an oil stove to cook by. The older children had left home by that time. She went to Hemyock School run by Mr. & Mrs. Prowse and cars fetched the children from outlying areas. A class was held in the Methodist Chapel and she remembers being taught there by Mrs. Holman, Miss Lee, and Mr. Paige who had come from London, probably with the evacuees.

They got on well with the evacuees, some of whom were billeted at Middle Mackham with a Mr. Carter. A former evacuee came to visit her recently. There was also at least one Italian prisoner-of-war working on the farm.

She went to the Baptist Chapel at Madford, now a private house, run by Mr. Doble and Mr. Cyril Ayres. She recalls the rationing, including bread rationing, and that they had hand-me-down clothing.

They used to walk to Hemyock to shop and had the choice of several shops. There were good shops in Uffculme, Longs who sold toys and dolls which she loved (and still does!), stockings and 1/- boxes of toffees. On special occasions they went to Taunton on the bus, return fare 1/9. They had very little in the way of entertainment, but she went to concerts by the Durham Light Infantry during the war.

During one very cold winter when the roads were impassable to vehicles, the milk churns were taken in wheelbarrows to a collecting point. Locals walked to Clayhidon to get bread from the baker and brought it back in pillowcases.

Roe Deer.

Eve

Kill or Cure

By modern standards health care in the Blackdowns was primitive, and folk remedies were frequently used. Times have come full circle and complementary medicine is now available at the Blackdown Practice. Here are some examples of earlier treatments

Scalded Daughter

One time Grandfather Manley was visiting a farmer on horse business and he asked the farmer's wife how the family were. She led him to her small daughter who was lying down and had a terrible scald on her leg, nearly through to the bone. This had been caused some weeks before by upsetting the kettle of boiling water from the open fire over her leg. The farmer's wife begged him to help.

He sent her to fetch a yellow and green leaf from the 'cattle cabbage'. This is the outside leaf of a vegetable found in gardens at that time. He heated this over the open fire on both sides until it went limp. Then he asked for fresh hog's lard which he smacked liberally onto both sides of the leaf. Next he asked the farmer's wife to bring a strip of old sheet. He used this to bandage the leaf and lard onto the child's leg.

When he went back to check on the child about a week later, she was no longer crying, she leapt up and threw her arms around his neck. He examined the wound and the flesh was beginning to grow back. He re-bandaged the leg and within two months it was completely healed.

He knew the plants growing in water or in bogs such as bladderwort, that could be used to heal rheumatism. These were rubbed into the skin, never too much or too little as the one would be ineffective and the other would be too much. Sometimes he was able to help people who were so crippled by rheumatism that they were in a wheelchair. After treatment the next time he saw them they only needed to use one stick!

Remedies for Colds

Mother used to make tea with elder blossoms. She would pick the elder flowers and lay them on newspaper to dry in the sun with some black currant leaves. When dry these would be put in a paper bag and hung in the chimney corner. Then if anyone had a cold mother would take a handful of these dried leaves and flowers and put in the tea pot to make tea. This tea would then be poured into a cup with a spoonful of golden syrup drunk hot and then the sufferer would go to bed. Another remedy for colds was tea made with black currant jam.

Ulcerated Legs

As a child I had very bad chicken pox. We had to get Dr. Hilliar up from Wellington who came by horse. He asked me "Have you laid any more eggs?"

There was a woman who suffered from ulcerated legs. She would send her daughter to collect pennywort leaves and violets from the hedgerows. She would then mix these with something she bought from the chemist to make an ointment and rub it on her legs to heal the ulcers.

Whooping Cough

We all had bad whooping cough - including my mother who became very ill - she nearly choked to death. As there were no telephones in those days we had to send a message down to Wellington for a doctor to visit. This took a long time.

Health visitor

A Health Visitor came to the school to examine each pupil. We were stripped to our waists and shoes and socks off. I had measles in my ears at 9 months old which caused my deafness and the Headmaster, Mr. Prowse, and his wife were advised to send me to a Deaf and Dumb School, but my parents were against sending me away. The Prowses kept me under their wings and taught me as a 'special pupil'.

Infections

We moved to Bolham, Burrow Hill where our only source of water was from a four inch drainpipe through a wall running continuously. Strangely enough when a thunderstorm was imminent the water would be very muddy. Consequently every year I would get a very bad throat infection and would be taken to Dr. Griffin (Senior). Once he took a swab as he thought it was diphtheria and I cried all the way home " I don't want to die". I had seen posters around picturing small children and stating "Diphtheria is deadly". Fortunately it turned out to be a quinsy.

Boils

One old neighbour was very embarrassed when she developed a boil in her groin. When she could no longer put off visiting the doctor she cut a piece out of her bloomers to expose the boil, and then after her visit to the doctor sewed it back in again!

Doctors remembered
Dr Laidlaw

My father, Dr. Laidlaw, was the local doctor from 1911-1945, and had surgeries in Uffculme, Willand, Kentisbeare and Westleigh as well as being doctor to the Mill and Friendly Societies. The women and children had to pay but as most of them couldn't afford it, he often visited free of charge. Panel patients paid 15/- a year and the District Nurse could be

had for 1d a week. Visits cost a guinea but the Vicar did not have to pay. The work was generally simpler, more personal and probably more demanding than today with mostly home visiting. My mother kept the books and did the prescriptions which were made up in the dispensary. The distinction between private and panel patients was marked, as private patients had their prescriptions wrapped in white paper beautifully sealed but the panel patients had theirs wrapped in newspaper. Commercial travellers called selling supplies.

Dr Huth

Hemyock before 1925 did not have its own resident doctor. Dr. Date of Culmstock attended patients in Hemyock until he left in 1912. He was succeeded by Dr. Sidney Huth, who was a well liked family doctor. He arrived in Culmstock from Bath in the 1912 and practised until early 1950. He was a familiar character driving around in his open topped car, with the hood always down whatever the weather. He wore a large white raincoat and smoked large cigars; his dog would ride with him, with front paws on the top of the windscreen. Children would gather outside his surgery when it was time for him to go on his rounds and he would tell them to jump in and take them for the ride.

Fred Coombes remembers the boys taking a crafty puff at the cigar when the doctor left it on the wall while visiting a patient. His favourite remedies were methylated spirits externally and castor oil internally. He died in 1956.

Clayhidon was served by doctors from Wellington, for example Drs. Meredith and Hillier. The late William Gill of Culmstock was stable boy for Dr. Hillier in his earlier career.

In 1925 a group of prominent villagers, deciding that Hemyock should have its own doctor, placed an advertisement. The doctor appointed was called Porter. The committee provided a house for him in Station Road. Dr. Porter, as they termed it, 'put up his plate'. This was not only illegal but was highly unethical and considered with contempt by established practitioners. Dr. Porter did not 'make a go of it' so he left to become a salaried Medical Officer in a colliery in Wales.

Dr John Griffin

Dr. John Griffin the 'First' worked hard for his family and to put his son through medical school at the Bristol General Hospital. He fell ill one day, was worse the next day, and on the third day died of pneumonia. This was not unusual in those pre-antibiotic days.

His son, also called Dr. John Griffin, worked as an Assistant to a Dr. Dixon in the slums of Southville, Bristol. But like so many young doctors and nurses in those days, he contracted TB. He was sent to a sanatorium in Switzerland by the philanthropic pioneer of the travel business, Sir Arnold Lunn. At the end of 1926 he had no capital available to buy a practice, as he had lost his own father before completing his medical degrees, so was looking for a cheap practice. He paid £100 in Hemyock having negotiated the price down from £120. In Dr. Griffin's first three months at Hemyock there was an epidemic of influenza and his receipts were £100 for which he was most grateful. At that time a surgery consultation fee was 2/6. to include a bottle of medicine. A visit was charged at 5/-. and a repeat bottle of medicine was 2/-. Arithmetic seems to show that the value put on the consultation was 6d.

The villagers provided a terraced house for Dr. Griffin and his wife next to James' egg packing station in Station Road. When they were expecting their first child they moved up to a house called then Sandhurst, next to The Manse. Consultations were held in the dining room and

patients waited on a bench in the hall. Later a consulting room and a tiny dispensary were built onto the side of the house at a cost of £120. The surgery had the sixth telephone in the district and when the automatic exchange was built the number became 206.

At first he rode a Douglas motor cycle, but soon acquired a Morris car, which was more in keeping with his new status. He became increasingly popular over a widening area with patients in Culmstock (not popular with Dr. Huth!), Blackborough, Sheldon, Dunkeswell (where he had a branch surgery), Clayhidon, Churchinford, Upottery, Luppitt and Yarcombe. He worked hard in the practice, which grew steadily. Later he developed an interest in giving anaesthetics, initially for dental extractions but later for general surgery.

On 14th August 1947 Dr. Thomas Logan, then aged 25, joined the practice. Dr. Griffin bought a building plot on the Culmstock Road to build a house and surgery, but with the inception of the National Health Service he was promoted to a position as consultant anaesthetist to the West Somerset group of hospitals. He survived to the age of 94! In 1958 Dr. John Lysaght Griffin the Third joined the practice.

Dr Logan

Dr. Logan was popular and much respected. He built the house known as Bean Close which contained a wing with Consulting Room, Dispensary and Waiting Room, with a separate entrance. In 1956 he formed a partnership with his friend and colleague, Dr. John Probyn of Churchinford. Tragically, in November 1966, Dr. Logan suffered a severe stroke which deprived him of speech. He was only 44 and never practised again. He died on 8th February 1983 aged 60. An oak tree is planted in his memory in Hemyock churchyard.

In 1955 Dr. Peter Hayne had been employed as an Assistant, but incompatibilities developed and Dr. Hayne took a single-handed practice in Carlisle, later moving back to Chilton Polden in Somerset.

The Dentist

Mr Farrant Senior, the dentist, came every Monday, on market day, to the cottage at the bottom of the High Street. Patients would sit in an old wooden chair and hold on because once he started pulling out a tooth he never let go until he had finished the job.

An Undertaker's Experience

A man came to our house to know if the firm would carry out a funeral as his old father had died. The family were living in a field on the left hand side of the road from Maidendown to the A38. The dwelling was a pit covered with galvanised iron. When father arrived to take particulars, the son had got the old man propped up against the hedge and was washing him down! As it was midwinter, rigor mortis soon set in! The son said he could not understand why the old man died as he was as fat as a pig!

Gypsy families have lived in the area for many years. Mrs Pike can remember when she was out walking to Sunday School at Symonsburrow with two other girls and they passed a gypsy house where a girl called Sophie had died. An old gypsy came out and asked them if they would like to come in and see Sophie in her coffin. She let the two older girls in but said that Mrs Pike was too young! Death was not always as dignified as it is today.

An 18 year old young lady died of TB at Hillmoor when there was deep snow and freezing weather. It was impossible to dig a grave in the churchyard, so they dug a tunnel in the snow and laid her there until the thaw set in.

53

A Happy Childhood

I looked forward to the summers when we went for picnics by the river. The picnic would be packed in a small brown leather suitcase with, of course, cucumber sandwiches. We would go for a paddle and my knitted swimsuit would stretch and be down to my knees when I got out.

A group of my mother's friends would have a day on the common blackberrying, armed with baskets and walking sticks to reach for the blackberries, the same leather suitcase, cricket bats and balls for the children to have a game of cricket.

My father had one day a week off, and if this fell on a Tuesday and we were on holiday from school, he would take us by train to Tiverton Market. I always looked forward to tea that day, as my mum would buy sausages from the butcher in Tiverton.

Living in the village, we used to get the fish man on Tuesday, and a man used to come on his bicycle and take orders for groceries to be delivered later in the week. The coalman came with his

horse and cart on Fridays. We would wait for the horse to move off, then out with a bucket and shovel! "Good for the roses" my father would say.

Christmas was a very happy family time. My uncle would cycle five miles to see me on Christmas Eve with a Christmas tree strapped to his cross bar. Whilst we decorated it and put up the trimmings, mother would be preparing supper of boiled ham and pickles made in the autumn. Friends would come round and we would sing around the piano and a friend would play the banjo.

I was fussy with my food and at Sunday breakfast I would only eat the yolk of my egg but my brother would eat the white. I loved the smell of ground coffee in the large green jug with a net cover over the top. My first banana sandwich was boiled parsnip mashed with banana essence!

Through the war there are such memories as picking up acorns for a farmer, I would get 3d a bucket and when he wasn't looking we would refill the bucket he had just emptied. We looked forward to the Americans coming to the village from Dunkeswell with sweets and chewing gum. We had a Christmas dinner once at the airfield and I came home and told my mother we had jam (cranberry sauce) with our turkey.

As a child, along with many others, I waited in the Village Square for Dr Huth to arrive after his surgery. He would go out on his rounds visiting his patients and take us in his big brown open car with the hood folded down. We would sit on the hood and one day, going over the bridge a boy fell off. We all had a good laugh.

❖ ❖ ❖

At school we would all take two tablespoons of golden syrup, some currants, raisins, two tablespoons of sugar and Mr. Prowse would make cakes and sweets. The ladies who served the tea would wear big white aprons and hats.

Happiest Days...?

Clayhidon School

We came to Clayhidon in December 1919 and I started school in January 1920. As I had already had two years schooling at Chideock, I was not classed as an Infant but a very small Junior, so I had to go into the 'Big Room' where the ages ranged from 6 to 14 years. I don't remember who my first teacher was, but the Headmistress was Miss Hamblyn.

She was only a small woman, but, my word, did she have a voice. She scared us all into obedience when she raised her tone. Not long after I started we had a new class teacher, Miss Dorothy Edwards (who most Clayhidon people knew as Mrs Percy Sanders of Hidonfields). It eased the situation quite a lot because Miss Hamblyn was then able to concentrate on the older pupils. The day started at 9.30a.m. as some children had a very long journey and in the winter they would have to leave home in the dark. The old school bell would start ringing about five minutes before lesson time to hurry up the dawdlers. The day started with the calling of the register followed by hymns and prayers and Bible reading until 10a.m. when the register would be checked for late comers and then the 3R's were well and truly drilled into us. I well remember chanting the tables each morning. It was such a bore but I have been thankful for it many times during my life. English was also a very strong point and we had English lessons in one form or another every day, either copying, essays or compositions. We were not allowed to write with pen and ink until we had full control of managing a pen. The ink wells were set in little holes in the desk

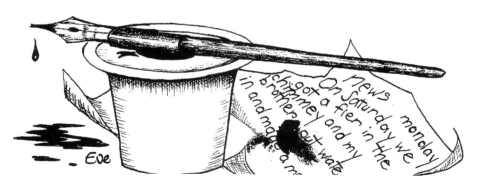

and refilled each week, so you can guess how much it was abused with blots on books and floor. Our fingers would get all inky if we dipped the pen too far into the inkwell.

One afternoon a week, usually Friday, we had singing lessons. We had no piano or any instrument of any sort, only a tuning fork. It always amazed me how she used to tap with the fork and then run down the scale until she hit the right note. Then we were away with such songs as 'Swanee River', 'Home Sweet Home', 'Hearts of Oak' and such like. Needlework was a favourite subject and we had lessons three times a week, two afternoons for sewing and one for knitting. The garments we made were more than shapeless, but the stitching had to be done exactly or we would have to take it out and do it all again.

I don't know what would be thought of the hygiene arrangements now, compared with conditions then. Our washing facilities were two zinc bowls set into a wooden bench in the back cloakroom with one roller towel which had to last from Monday to Friday. So you can well imagine what it was like by Friday with 60 or 70 children using it. We couldn't drink the water that came from the washing tap, but from the pump situated at the back of the building, and we drank from a communal cast iron cup, which was securely fastened to the pump casing by a length of chain... Ugh!

The toilets were flushed with a general supply of water from a large tank with a ball cock arrangement to regulate the flow at intervals, but never when it was needed!

The Attendance Officer arrived each week to check up on absentees. He was Mr. Percy Blamey and he cycled from Cullompton and visited all the valley schools on the way up. The curriculum was much the same over the years and in May 1927, Miss Hamblyn left Clayhidon to be married in Durham Cathedral, to a childhood sweetheart. After that we had another mistress for a few weeks and then a master took over until the end of term. After the summer holidays we had another master for a few weeks until Miss Hayter was installed as a permanent Head Teacher. I was sorry when I finished at Christmas 1927 but I was needed at home

❖

I was made a prefect and was responsible for the younger children. One very naughty little girl climbed the apple tree and wouldn't come down. I was frightened that Miss Hayter would hold me responsible.

❖

❖

When I first went to school there were no cars in Clayhidon. I think the first car was owned by Mr. Bennison from Applehayes. When we heard it coming, we would all rush to the wall at the end of the playground to see it pass by. It was so exciting!

❖

as my mother did not enjoy very good health. I admit to a few tears at the thought of leaving school where I had spent so many happy hours.

I went to school in Clayhidon from 5-14 years. The lane was narrow with rough stone chippings and I still bear the scars on my knees from falls. The stones were terribly hard on our feet and our shoes. We walked to school, of course, in all weathers. There were three teachers. The little ones were taught in the room which is now the Village Hall kitchen. The remaining pupils were divided into two classes - taught in the same large room without any divider - one teacher at either end. When I first went to school, Miss May was the Infant Teacher, Miss Edwards taught the middle age group and Miss Hamblyn was the Head Teacher. She lived in the house attached to the school and had a lovely dog called Topsy. Sometimes we were allowed to play with Topsy and made a great fuss of her.

Due to illness we had a 'stand in' teacher - Mrs. Hutchins. The children wouldn't do what she told them and they were very naughty. Mrs. Hutchins left, and they sent a man teacher, Mr. Stewart, to restore order. Mr. Stewart was very strict and wacked the girls and boys very hard on their hands. One of the little Wittrow girls was so upset by her beating that she locked herself in the lavatory and wouldn't come out. However, order was eventually restored! Miss Hayter became Head. She was an exceptional teacher. She started yearly outings for us, to the sea, and a Christmas Party when each child was given a present from the tree.

Of course there were no school dinners so we took a sandwich. When I was older during the war, the Government provided a thick type of cocoa for all children.

During the same period, in the 1920's, there was a small private school for girls at Caller's farm, Clayhidon, run by Mrs Maynard. Here are some letters written by the girls, probably as a class exercise.

Callers Farm
Clayhidon
June 6ᵗʰ 1923

Dear Fay,
Betty was very pleased to have
a letter addressed to her. She stood
at her chair when she first came in
and stared at it, then rolled her eyes.
What a pity you did not take
your bathing costume.
I hope you are enjoying
your self. The other day I
thought the rabbet would die; it sat
down all day long. On Sunday when
Marian came and she said it would
die too. But it has revived now. The
bantams are looking quite ugly now they have
got feathers sticking out all over. I hope
Mrs Lang and Mary are quite well. Mr Brealy's
horse is a beauty, William Gill passes through
the yard every day with it. All the ammials send
their love and me too. Mother and I
went to Smythes on Monday evening.

Love
Fram
Queenie

School
June 6ᵗʰ 1923

Dear Miss Maynard
I hope that you are enjoying
yourself at the sea. How do you like it? Mamie and
and I are learning a piece out of "Hiawatha's
Fishing." Kitty brought her dolly to school yesterday and
forgot to take it and this morning she said to me, "I
have left Rosie at school!". Rosie is sitting on the
school room table with a gold band round her hair.
Yesterday Olive went to Strawbridges Farm to see
Aunty and she rode her biciyle and she let me try
to ride it, she only pushed the seat while I was
guiding. Then I met Mummie with the horse + trap and
a little lamb and she drove me home.
Your affectionate pupil Florrie.

Composition
Dear Miss Maynard
I have
finished the Sequel
I took home my
exercise book on Monday
I am getting on with
money sums. Do you
like this writing? I
have done some in my
exercise book. With love
Vera

Round about 1931, Jack and his sister went to school in Hemyock and then in Clayhidon with Miss Hamlyn and Miss Hayter. Jack recalls going to the teacher's house to listen to the wireless for the first time. They had to be in school by 8.45 a.m. after a long walk and having helped with the milking and farm other jobs first. Some children walked from Jacob's City near the Harriers. They cooked raw potatoes on the school stove for dinner and after school faced a long walk home again with the older children often carrying the younger ones.

Smoking was not allowed at school and if caught, an offender suffered the Headmaster's standard punishment. The pupil was made to smoke a very strong cigar - right through - a bucket was placed near at hand!

Hemyock School in 1916

I came to Hemyock during the first World War. I went to Hemyock school. It was an old school, not the one by the church. We had a school master called Baxter who was the first school master at the school after it was built. There used to be a bell on the roof that was rung about five minutes before the school time, and everyone knew very well that they had to be in school when the bell rang or there would be trouble.

Some long time later when they did the roof of School Court they wanted things tidied up. In the bicycle shed amongst the clearing up I found the bell clapper. I said to my wife, I wouldn't mind giving Mr. Richardson, the schoolmaster, some money for the old bell as it was sentimental to me you see. Mr. Richardson had a school sale, and he was told that I was interested. I said I would give him £7 for the old bell and he was delighted. I had that bell for a long time, but I wasn't happy as I felt it should belong to the village, so I contacted the schoolmaster at the new school, and said "Would you like the bell presented to the school?." He jumped at the idea. But I stipulated that it was never to leave Hemyock and never to be sold. A nice oak fitting was made by Richard Hart's carpenter for it and it is now hanging up at the school

Hemyock School in the 1930s

These memories of the Primary School are of 60 years ago.

My first clear memory was of being taken into the arms of Mrs. Prowse teacher and wife of our Head. My mother explained that I was left handed thought to be a fault in those days. Mrs. Prowse assured me that I would not be retrained to become right handed.

At school there was the same Headmaster for the whole time I was there, Mr. Percy H. Prowse, called (not in his hearing) "Perp", and who could blame us... his wife always called him that. There were originally three classrooms now forming the front part of Old School Court. As numbers grew, wooden classrooms were placed in the playground. Mr. Prowse, at first, had no telephone thus protecting him from tiresome parents and Education Officers. He had no secretary, typewriter or office and taught full time. He lived in the School House, so we saw him out and about.

At lunch times we had a lot of freedom and could wander all over the village without supervision. Remember though there was far less traffic then, only a few horse and carts went down to the Milk Factory. The coke was delivered to the school by horse and cart. Mr. Dennis Pring called each morning with his tiny bottles of milk; in the winter we had to warm them by the coke-fired stove. I have hated milk ever since then!

What did I learn at school? Looking back I feel that I was taught to seek knowledge and to be a useful person - a 'good citizen' perhaps. I cannot recall arithmetic lessons (OK maths to you younger lot). Mr. Prowse taught geography, and I retain a deep interest in the wider world and its people. History was in the care of Mr. Robinson - a young man, clearly talented. I disliked him, but he must have made an impression on me because if you look at the hundreds of books I

possess, you will find they are mostly historical. Mrs. Prowse taught art, which consisted mostly of drawing "still life", e.g. an apple. We were taught to emphasise the highlights - and all this was done in chalk. Mr. Prowse was a keen gardener, and in what is now part of the children's play area we had a fine school garden. On my patch, my 'boss' was a slightly older pupil - Mr. Ray Casely - a splendid chap as he was so patient with the younger less experienced pupils. Mr. Prowse was very keen on a 'fine tilth' - a point which drove me to much impatience. Looking after my garden now, very little fine tilth is seen. We helped to plant the trees along Culmbridge Road, and I often stand and gaze at their beauty.

We didn't do a lot of sports, to my relief, as I was never a team person. I recall the colourful may pole, which was taken out of store once a year.

Another item adorning 'top-class' was a set of boards for 'Best boy and girl of the year'. We had to vote and I recall one year when we were bribed with sweets by a boy who keenly desired the title. I took the sweets and then voted for my real friend - George Bale. I cannot remember if the briber achieved his desired result

- I hope not!

We had treats; we were taken to Taunton to see Snow White and the Seven Dwarfs - wonderful! In school we saw a flickering cine film of the Canadian Pacific Railways.

My school days were happy ones - one tends to forget the difficult bits - a visit from the school dentist and so on. I can still see the 'bug nurse' - nothing changes.

I had a pair of crepe soled shoes that squeaked as I walked with deep embarrassment. I used to stand in a stream at Culm Davy hoping the water would still the sound but it never did. One of the many things about growing old is that one doesn't worry about such small things.

On 3rd September 1939 my school changed! We had a small group of pupils from a Catholic School in the East End of London, with their smart teacher Miss de Lacey. Her grand outfits caused the local lady teachers to look to their laurels. We boys had the pick and tough luck on the local girls, for now we had a large group of girls from a school in Edmonton. I recall Gabrielle and her lovely long, red hair and my 'true love' Betty Moore but she dropped me when I joined the Army and wrote a 'Dear John' letter.

With an influx of so many children from the bombs in London, we had to extend the school and use the Methodist Church and the Church Rooms. 'We used to walk there in 'crocodiles'. Seated with me at my desk was Mrs. Rosemary Perrott - then Rosemary Salter - she had an unfailing sense of humour - something she has never lost.

Did you know that girl pupils of Hemyock School, over 75 years ago, used to spend a week in the Church Room tackling what we would now call domestic science; washing and ironing, cooking on a range? How on earth was this managed? There would not have been electricity and no laid on water and the kitchen and present toilets didn't exist.

Few children had watches 75 years ago; pupils walking to school from Culm Davy and Whitehall used to check the time from the rooks at the top of Blackpit Hill. Not only were watches in short supply but swimming costumes when mixed bathing took place below Brookfields.

When I retired, Hemyock School invited me to lend a hand. The tiny part I play gives me enormous pleasure - each Friday morning, my welcome is warm and happy. The young pupils are super (a word not used when I went

At school Miss Aggar was very good. At Easter each year, she gave each pupil a present and one year we had an egg made of scented soap.

One Christmas we did a pantomime 'Robin Hood' and the younger ones did 'Little Nut Tree'

to school). The teachers are under much pressure - yet give so much of their time to helping the future.

On the wall of one of the classrooms at Hemyock Primary School, was a huge board bearing the names of pupils who had won the Good Fellowship Prize in the past. To introduce the procedure of voting to the children in the top class, a polling booth was set up, as for real, and boy pupils voted for the boy they thought had behaved as a Good Fellow throughout the year, and the girls did likewise. In my last year at school along with Percy Moon, I won it and we were taken by our headmaster, Mr Prowse to Mr Melhuish. After a short speech on how to go forward in life, he presented us each with the princely sum of a £1 note. A proud moment, as I had never been given one before. Decision time - what to spend it on!

We did not have to step out of line or else the cane was shown to us and one or two boys were often in trouble. The highlight of the year was preparing for sports day. For weeks we learnt may pole dancing and country dancing in the playground. I remember one day Mr Prowse said "Here comes Lloyd Drake with his Queen Marys on". Of course he meant hob nailed boots. Quite a few boys wore them, thumping around.

Denis was educated first at Hemyock School and then passed the scholarship to go to Tiverton Grammar School. At home he behaved well because Father's word was law but was less amenable at school. He was made the 'bellboy' but when the class had been noisy one day he was told to 'sit still' when he tried to go ring the bell. Undeterred, he told the teacher that he had a job to do and was going to do it and went! The Master caught up with him at milk break and Denis 'happened' to flick his milk over the poor man's suit. For this he had to learn one theorem a day for a week.

Culmstock School

I will always remember the big round coal stove in each of the three classrooms with fireguards around them. In wet weather the children who had come a long distance would have their clothes put on the fireguards to dry and older children would take it in turns to stoke the fires. Everybody walked to school from as far as Red Ball and Lane End, and I think there were two who rode their ponies. At one time Horlicks was provided in the morning for a ha'penny a day.

There were three classes; Mr. Bull took the top class (he was the headmaster from 1917-1952 and we always called him Gaffer). Of course he lived in School House as the headmasters always did. Miss Harris (later Mrs. Kerslake) taught needlework and would make the girls unpick their stitches many times until she was satisfied. Mrs. Huth, who taught singing, was very strict but was so pleased with us when we went to a singing festival in Exeter and got second prize.

The Greedy family walked from Red Ball. When horses were carting stones for road laying they would rush out from school to get a lift home on the carts. They loved horses and would help drive them. There would be birds' nests in the hedges all the way down from Woodgate; and going home they would climb trees, go bird nesting, wander across fields. They would run through the tidy piles of stones at the side of the road which had been piled up neatly by the stone breakers and scatter them.

We went to Culmstock School and we would hear the school bell ringing and would run like hell down the hill to get there before it stopped. If I was lucky I got a a lift down to school in a pony and trap with Mr. Bill Tucker who farmed at Frys Farm when he took his milk down to Dairy Court. We took a sandwich for dinner and there was a big white enamel jug of hot cocoa to go with it, it was good stuff too! I can remember doing a cross stitch embroidery in shades of blue, I was sent to show it to Mr. Bull and he was very impressed.

I can remember the day Kitty Kerslake started teaching at Culmstock School, she was very strict about getting the sewing right and we were made to pick it out if it wasn't just so. I couldn't see to do it as I always had poor sight and was always getting in trouble so my father went to see Mr. Bull, the Headmaster. I didn't have to do the sewing after that. Mrs. Huth used to come to school to play the piano and teach us singing Jerusalem was one of the songs we used to sing. We had school outings each year on the train, always to Teignmouth.

Smeatharpe School

We would lean over the railings for candy, gum and lifesavers from the US servicemen at Smeatharpe, They invited us to a party at the American Camp at Willand.

Along with several of the village children, I attended Smeatharpe School. I used to ride on the back of mother's bicycle. We would walk as far as a certain oak tree up Red Lane and then get on. Happily the tree is still there!

Every Friday afternoon the Dowager Viscountess Sidmouth (who was then in her 80's and one of the old school) would visit. After she was escorted in and settled by her chauffeur she would call the register, to which we all stood and replied individually "Present my lady" and then we sang hymns to her. She died in the early fifties.

Churchstanton School

I went to Churchstanton School when I was five. We walked to school in all weathers. There were two teachers, the Head who was called Mrs. Cronin, and another teacher, Miss Moore, in two classrooms. I won a prize of a fountain pen for the best piece of writing. I was so proud of that pen. We had school dinners which I enjoyed. My mother paid 1/10 a week.

When I was at Churchstanton school, we were convinced that an old woman living in a cottage was a witch. She was called Netta Jennings and was dirty and bent over. Her cottage had a tin roof and we used to throw stones onto the roof, and were terrified when she came out in anger.

Years later I visited her and found she was harmless and really a dear old soul - not a witch at all.

When we moved house I attended Smeatharpe School, and then Honiton School for one term and I left school at fourteen.

Dunkeswell School

Mostly I remember being cold! Mrs. Driver would light the stove in the morning and when it was time to go home it would just be getting warm. One thing I shall never forget was Donald Stevens fell over in the playground and had an awful graze on his knee, and the teacher just tipped iodine on it. The poor boy hit the roof.

Private Education

My two brothers went to prep. school in Burnham and on to Rugby but I was taught at home by two governesses, Edith and Nellie White. Edith taught me the piano and Nellie taught me until I was twelve when I went away to school in Burnham. In the 1930's I was 'finished' with nine months at Malvern and later in London to learn German and then to Vienna.

I went to Freiburg-in-Bresgau in 1938 only to discover that people were beginning to be rude to the British and that there were many tanks around. I joined FANY and learned how to strip an engine and drive in convoy.

❖

Most children went to the Council School until fourteen, then went out to work. The bright ones who had passed the scholarship went on to Middle Schools, later called Grammar Schools, in Tiverton.

❖

❖

We used to go to school at Tiverton by train, changing at Tiverton Junction. Evan Howells, the Station Master, would keep the train waiting if we were late, and at the right time of the year we would pick apples off the trees as we passed Southey Barton.

❖

Education reflected the great class divide. There were a number of other private schools like that at Callers Farm. There was a Dame School, in Craddock, run by Miss Hancock, who was Montessori trained and an excellent teacher. She had about 15 pupils, the boys staying till 8 or 9 and the girls till 11, when they went off to boarding school, some doing very well academically, with several boys getting major scholarships to Oxford and Cambridge.

Tiverton Grammar Schools

At the age of twelve I attended Tiverton Girls Grammar School. I rushed to the train each morning at 7.20 and arrived home at 5p.m. We had navy blue uniforms and pale blue blouses and always had to wear hats, berets in winter and panamas in summer. We walked in file from Tiverton station to the school and when war broke out we had to carry our gas masks as well as our cases.

For some children it was not an easy journey by train to school. Donald Salter spent most journeys under the seat or in the luggage rack which were then made like a hammock of very strong twine. Denis was pushed by someone into the window in the carriage door which broke. Of course his father was kept in the dark and Denis had to pay for the repair himself. There were only two carriages on the train so the girls and boys had to travel separately. Undeterred, the Hemyock boys were able to get out of the door and climb along the wooden running board into the girls' carriage.

War on the Door Step

The airfield at Dunkeswell took about four years to build and was finished in 1942. When the airfield was built, lorry load after lorry load of stones was brought in. Dunkeswell airfield was built first, then Smeatharpe and then Trickey Warren. Before D-Day Dakotas could be seen pulling gliders around all day. President Kennedy's older brother took off from Dunkeswell and no more was seen of him.

In 1941 I was farming over at Moorhayes, milking in the cowstall, when Yorkie Lowman came down in a bit of a flap, a little excited. As he was coming down over Moorhayes Hill there was a huge barrage balloon in the road just by the entrance to Hurst Farm, with a lot of wire ropes. We told P.C. Stokes of Hemyock and he informed the Army who had it removed. On another occasion, I was going to Wides in Hemyock with 15 dozen eggs, and a German plane came over Moorhayes House. I could see the swastika as plain as anything, and I think it was on a reconnaissance flight over Dunkeswell aerodrome. After a couple of nights three bombs were dropped, two at Abbey Mill Farm at Dunkeswell Abbey, and the other one in Little Mead at Lower Mackham Farm. This bomb went down about 35 feet. The Army dug down and shored it up, they took the fuse out and we towed the bomb out across the field with a Fordson tractor. The field was so wet that the lorry couldn't get down there, but the Army lorry took it away, sorted it out, then brought it back to Gilbert Forbear at Mackham and the bomb was in his barn for years and is now in the Museum at Honiton. The other two bombs that dropped that night were on the other side of the river and they made lovely duck ponds! The next night three more bombs were dropped, one landed right behind Mr. Forbear's farmhouse at Lower Mackham House, shattering the windows and making a mess of some tiles. It killed one of our cows when the shrapnel went into its side. A Liberator crashed on the Dunkeswell Abbey road and made a mess of the hedges by Dunkeswell Abbey Chapel.

One night we were going to a dance, and I picked up a Yank airman and took him to Kilmington to the dance. When we arrived back at Dunkeswell airfield he gave me three pairs of Wellington boots. This was at a time when coupons were needed for clothes. He asked me how much gasoline I could get, I told him we could get a couple of gallons to go to church. I went up to the Aerodrome the next morning and he filled up some jerry cans with gasoline, and not an eyelid was blinked. We used to pick up the swill from the canteen at the airfield, and the Americans used to put 7lb tins of ice cream for us under the swill.

I was able to get as much petrol as I liked, from a local cattle dealer, in two colours pink or white, the pink being for business. I used to sieve the pink through my gas mask, but when I realised perhaps the gas mask would be needed for my own use, and probably be made useless, I had to

find another way to strain the petrol. The best way to get rid of the pink dye was to cut the top off a large loaf of bread, scoop out a pat and slowly strain it through. It would take a week to get a gallon going drip, drip, and 90% of the dye came out. This is how I used to spend my Sunday afternoons.

We would incorporate work with our pleasure. I remember going to Culmstock to pick up some plants, going home round Hembury Fort way, parking in the Kings Arms car park in Honiton, changing into our dancing clothes and off to a dance for a couple of hours. There were always plenty of dances to go to. One night I went to a dance with a band called the Savannah Dance Band, another night the Ambassadors Band. Eddie Selway would sit playing his accordion, with his eyes shut and a cigarette hanging out of the side of his mouth, with his carpet slippers on and Roy Tucker used to play his saw. Ordinary dances used to be 2/-, Young Farmers dances were 2/6, but if you were in the Home Guard, in uniform with your great big army boots, you could get in for half price.

At the beginning of the war, volunteers were asked to come forward to help with the war effort. Three or four of us used to go and stand on top of a hedge at Windsor Cross with a two pronged dung pick, for what purpose I don't know. A little later we were given uniforms and then we were upgraded to the Home Guard. We were given rifles but no bullets, what good would that do! Dougie Pike who was a dispatch rider, would come down and call us up about two or three in the morning. A farmer had a smallholding with about five or six cows, and said he couldn't come one night because he had a cow calving. This happened five times, and the Commanding Officer said "You've only got five cows and this is the sixth night you have had off".

One night I went with a chap in an old Austin van over to Luppit Common rabbit shooting and I shot fourteen. We drove home past Jacks House where Oswald Mosely was interned. P.C. Stokes from Hemyock was there, and waved us down but fortunately he was on the Smeatharpe side of the road and we saw him in time to slip round the other way. A lucky escape!

We had two Italian prisoners of war at one time to help us as we had a lot of work to do. They would bring their own bread and cheese, and if we had a lot of work to finish we would ring up the Commandant at Waterloo Cross where they stayed to tell him we would be keeping them for a little longer than usual. The prisoners were happy to stay and work. When they saw a black cloud they would say "aqua" meaning "rain".

During the war we had about 80 or 90 acres. The War AG Committee gave the instructions and told us how much land we had to plough up, depending how much acreage we owned. How much to cut, how much to plough, with perhaps an acre of potatoes and the rest had to be sown with corn. We got our seed drills and other machinery from Mr. Blackmore's farm. We could keep as many animals as we liked, and produce as much milk as we could. If we upped our milk production we were given a printed certificate, and if we upped it 20% we were given a bigger certificate.

After the war about fourteen children used to walk to school from Stentwood, and I put a fowl house up at Gypsy Cross for the children to shelter in the wet weather. It was accidentally burnt down when the scrub was burnt. I put up another fowl house and that shelter is still there today. We put orange boxes for the children to sit on, and later someone put a settee up there. Sometimes children would ride bikes and leave them there while at school, but after one was stolen nobody did that any more.

For King and Country

I wonder if, besides myself, there is anyone left in Clayhidon who can remember a soldier in red, sitting in the porch of his cottage polishing his buttons on his scarlet tunic. On Sunday afternoons, he would appear in his red uniform, a gorgeous figure, still upright even though he must have been very old. Two world wars have come and gone since the old soldier sat there polishing his buttons.

First World War Memories

The First World War was declared on August 4th and a recruiting officer came to Hemyock in 1916, looking for recruits to go to war. The Post Office subscribed to a telegram of War News and the Post Mistress would appear in Uffculme Square ringing a bell to announce the latest news.

❖ ❖ ❖

In the 1st world war there was much loss of life as seen by the well tended war memorials in the villages.

One father went to war at the beginning of 1917. It was a very upsetting experience for the family with three children. He went into the Royal Engineers but stayed in this country, going first to Southsea and then on to Kent, helping with the building of England's defences to keep out the Germans.

❖ ❖ ❖

Joan's uncle was serving in the army fighting in Germany. One day he was chasing the Germans through a shell shattered house, and on through the garden where he came upon a doll lying on the ground. He wasn't married, therefore had no children of his own, but he thought of his niece, Joan. He picked up the doll and put it in his rucksack. Her uncle carried it with him until he came home on leave. The doll was about 15 inches tall with a china face, the body was fully jointed, even the fingers and toes. The clothes had to be replaced, but the doll always had a French air about it. It is still treasured by the family.

✧ ✧✧ ✧

When Vic Bale came home he brought two big shell cases with him, which were sewn into the lining of his great coat. He came through the Customs on arriving in England and his kit bag needed checking out. He put his great coat over a chair as they checked his kit bag, then picked up his coat with his kit bag and came home. Dora has those shell cases on her mantelpiece today. The great coat had its lining sewn up with blanket stitch, and is still up in the loft.

✧ ✧✧ ✧

My grandmother had quite bit of bunting. There were trees around the garden at Callers at that time, so the bunting was hung all around the garden. In the morning they were on the Rectory lawn!! All children were given a little flag by Squire Harrison. He lived at Applehayes, Clayhidon as an artist and was founder of the Camden School of Painters.

Second World War Memories

Home Guard

Calls to serve the flag in the 2nd world war were answered by enrolling voluntarily in the Home Guard.

The Home Guard at Clayhidon and Hemyock was a large organisation. They were on a rota for guard duty at night. They had their own H.Q. hut. They were not like Dad's Army - but in spite of their efficiency, it was rumoured that one night when they were on duty they were frightened out of their wits, and it turned out to be only a loose horse. It gave them a scare and the horse nearly got itself shot!

The Home Guard organised the Dances in the Club Room at the Half Moon, I suppose to keep

✧

The Great War ended at 11a.m. on November 11th 1918. An armistice was celebrated sometime after. Our cousin, having returned from Palestine, climbed up the monkey tree and put a flag on the top. What scratches he had on his arms! Not war wounds!

✧

order. The Home Guard went out every night, and one night two men went down to the Whitehall Halt and sat down on the seat in the station waiting room. A friend had the garden behind the Whitehall House, and they saw that he had a lovely lot of cauliflowers. "We'll have one or two of them", they said, so they went and cut the cauliflowers, brought them back and put them under the seat. Just before they were going home, who should come in the waiting room but the Hemyock policeman to have a chat. They stayed there until they could stay no longer. What should they say about the cauliflowers? In the end they said that the owner had given them the cauliflowers and then later they had to tell the man that they had taken them!

Another night they were on duty down at the Whitehall Halt. What could they have tonight? So they went up to a farmer who had swedes. They cut some and went up several nights taking the swedes. One of them had bought a hedge of wood from the farmer so they decided to go and see him, and pay for it. After they paid for the hedge, he gave them some swedes and said "It looks as though them gypsies have been down here, they have cleared nearly half the field!"

Home Guard, Culmstock

At the beginning of the war, the Local Defence Volunteers was formed, and affectionately known as Look, Drop and Vanish, later it became the Home Guard. In the early days of the war, the volunteers were issued with an armband, a gas mask and a tin helmet, and had to provide their own weapons; pitchforks, shotguns or whatever was available. Early officers were Mr. Cubitt, Mr. Lowry and Jimmy Collier, and Bill Alford remembers joining at sixteen. As the war advanced, weapons and uniforms were supplied.

Rifle practice took place at Hembury Fort. Dennis Hoile remembers scoring five bulls at one practice and feeling very pleased. Hand grenade practice took place at Maidendown. John Knowlman recalled a cover being put over the hole in the top of Culmstock Beacon hut and two bunks being installed to make a guard hut, another guard hut was behind the Farrant's bungalow at Westown.

Bill Gill and Sammy Burroughs had draped ivy round their helmets and shoulders to patrol the Beacon area. They challenged Mrs. Simpson of Scotts Shute as she collected firewood "Halt, who goes there?" and got the reply "Be you two off your heads?"

One night patrol on the Beacon spotted something white, moving slowly every now and then. They crept round and viewed it from every angle, and when they eventually advanced and challenged they discovered it was only a white paper bag! Further up the valley some Home Guards were similarly puzzled by something or somebody slowly advancing and breathing heavily on a very dark night. After opening fire they discovered that they'd shot a farmer's horse. Two of them challenged Dennis Seaford when he was walking on the railway lines one evening; being over zealous they locked him in the railway hut. One night, about 1,000 troops carried out an exercise on the Beacon, the men on guard duty didn't know they were there until one of them came out of the hut for a 'wee'.

Evacuees

The first big impact of the Second World War was the arrival of the evacuees. A bus laden with

school children, who had just waved tearful farewells to grieving parents in London's East End, made the journey through the sombre city to Paddington and thence to an unknown destination. Eventually the train pulled up at Tiverton Station, and the children with their teachers and escorts marched through the town to the Pannier Market where kind W.V.S. Ladies were waiting with tea and sandwiches for all.

Dispersal time came. The party of 114 children was detailed to a coach carrying them to Culmstock where they were ushered into the school. It was heartening to see kind faces of the local people waiting to welcome them into their homes, as children and grown-ups alike were feeling decidedly jaded by this time. Gradually the children were allotted homes by Mr. E. Farmer, the billeting officer, and the six teachers watched the tiny ones, holding tightly on to older brothers and sisters, going off with their new friends. Next day back in the Village Hall, they were sorted out into age groups. The party had been made up of children from several schools in the Bethnal Green area, which made academic assessment difficult. Classes for the evacuee children were held in various places. Children were taught for several months in the Village Hall kitchen. The weather during those summer months was incredibly dry and warm so afternoon school was often held in a field kindly lent by Mr. H. Luxton. There was very little equipment and they were dependent on Mr. Bull, the headmaster, and his school for supplies. Eventually the evacuees and local children were amalgamated into new classes within the school and Village Hall.

Until more equipment arrived, several afternoons the entire evacuee group walked up to Culmstock Beacon, carrying sacks to fill with sphagnum moss, which grows in the damp areas there. They were then carried down to Tapscott House, to be sent away and used for medical purposes in the war effort.

An entry in the Culmstock School log-book for July 8th, 1940, states:- 'Seven evacuated children absent from school this afternoon.' Later they were brought into school by P.C. Stokes of Hemyock, who had found them about half a mile the other side of Hemyock, having run away from their billets they started to walk to London. Indeed, a poignant indication of the disruptive effect of wartime on the lives of young children.

We had four evacuees, who arrived with a billeting officer and portable single beds, like stretchers, and one blanket. What fun we all had - being free to run on 60 acres - climb trees, play at the river, catch the horses and ride in the trap. Just before bedtime we would play darts or hide and seek in the barns. At hay making and harvest too, trying to catch rabbits that had run to the centre of the field. The reaper left stubble about 6 inches high which was so painful on the legs as only skirts or dresses were worn.

Vera Kerslake remembers a young boy being brought down to Southey Barton at 10 o'clock at night as Mr. Farmer couldn't find anyone to take him in. Mercy Seaford recalls how happy she and Gladys Quick were when they had evacuees as it meant they had someone to play with.

One family still has a white marble clock which evacuees with mother accompanying them left behind when they returned to London.

Odette Sansom (Churchill) came to lodge at Mrs. Balsom's cottage at Red Ball in 1941. Her three daughters came with her and she would walk into the village to do her shopping, groceries at Strawbridges and meat at Fishers. She was later a secret agent and suffered torture at the hands of the Germans.

Story of an Evacuee

I was a young evacuee from South Acton, W.3. and came to a wonderful place of fields, woods, rivers and streams. I was billeted with the kindly Mr. and Mrs. W. Redwood at 4, Broadway. I used to ride on his bus to pick up the Irish workers who were building Dunkeswell Aerodrome. They were in billets in the village. One vivid memory was of going up Lemons Hill, following a rare delivery of rationed chocolate, a box or two had fallen off and had left a trail of broken pieces waiting to be picked up and eaten.

I can remember skinning moles to sell at 4d a skin and collecting acorns to sell to Mr. W. Drake the Butcher to feed to his pigs which were kept behind the Sunday School, next to the slaughterhouse. I helped wash down the cattle market after the Monday Auction of livestock.

Some of the animals came by train to Hemyock Station, and were driven up to the market as there were not many cattle lorries then. The pub was always busy and stalls were set up selling farm tools, harness; a really busy day for the village. The village policeman was on duty at the Pump. I earned a few pennies helping to drive cattle by road to one or other of the local farms, and was let out of school to help with farm work, like potato picking. This was a great time, we were paid 3d an hour. Other wartime work for schools was gathering foxglove leaves and rose hips, both used for medicines.

After our house in London had been bombed, my Mother and I lived in part of the farmhouse at Burrow Hill Farm. Some farmers in the area had groups of either German or Italian P.O.W.'s to work on the farms. One morning four or five Italians came to gather the apples in the orchard where my Mother was hanging out the washing and singing while she worked. My Mother had a very good voice, and as she was singing one of Italy's popular songs, "O Sole Mio" in Italian it moved the prisoners to tears and they dropped their buckets and ran to speak to her in their native tongue. It must have been a morning to remember for them, they were not much more than boys. A surprising twist to this story is that my Father was in the British Army in the West Desert R.A.

S.C. D.R. and able to converse in Italian; he was asked to interpret for the newly captured prisoners.

Children's Contribution

Children were expected to make a contribution to the war effort
Collecting:-
Acorns for pig farms.

Stinging nettles which were dried on string lines - to use like tobacco.
Making underclothes from parachutes - wonderful silk.
Rose hips for babies' Rose Hip Syrup.
Scraps for chickens - your own or someone in the village.
Blackberrying for jam - W.I. was given sugar to make jam for the community - hence their image which still remains of all 'Jam and Jerusalem'.
Picking and collecting fruit - special holidays for potato harvest
Nuts.
Paper, tins, old iron, saucepans.
Brown paper bags for shopping plus a basket as shops didn't supply bags or wrapping paper.
Foxglove seeds and dried leaves for treating heart disorders
Envelopes, which were reused with sticky labels until they finally fell to bits and were discarded.

A Teenager's Memory

As a youngster at boarding school I spent holidays twice a year in Northern Ireland where my father was stationed, by a lake where they tested spent torpedoes. I travelled on my own from the age of fourteen to Northern Ireland by sea through seas peppered with U boats. I was surprised, the first time I visited Northern Ireland, to see men serving in the shops, as this was most unusual at this time in England. I also went across the border into Southern Ireland. Here the culture shock was enormous: brightly lit streets, no blackout of houses or trains, plentiful food and the Nazi flag flying over the German Embassy.

At boarding school we were expected to help the war effort by knitting for the services. All girls and women throughout the U.K. were encouraged to do this. Wool in Service colours came from a central government source for wool scarves, balaclava helmets, fishermen's jerseys and socks, flying boot socks. The girls at my school had to take their knitting with them everywhere and were even expected to knit during the lull in meal times between the first and second course! It was customary for all knitters to attach a label with their name and address to the completed garments and it was very exciting to get a letter from a service man who was wearing something that you had made, although for security reasons it was always sent without an address.

There were black G.I.'s and white G.I.'s later in the war. When one seventeen year old got off the train on her way home from work in the evenings, the black G.I.s would be sitting on the wall outside the Methodist Chapel - at first she just smiled and later passed the time of day. She still remembers how polite they were and how surprised they were that a white girl spoke to them. They came to the village whist drives.

Sonny Farmer came round to tell us who had to join up and who would be deferred. He also said what ground had to be ploughed up and what had to be planted. As a girl I had to help on the farm and I remember ploughing up pieces of meadow under the Beacon. I had to plough right out to the edge and would pretty well get the horse up in the hedge to do it. There was a copse below our farm being cleared with horses dragging timber. After the terrible way I saw the horses treated, hitting them to make them haul out the wood, I never want to see working horses come back.

After France collapsed in 1940, Churchill and General Sikorski decided that the Polish Army would come to England and fight from England. So we landed in Plymouth dressed as Frenchmen and with French military tanks and put up in a centre for admissions and counting. The ladies there made everyone a cup of tea but the men said "What is that?" and were told it was a cup of tea made with powdered milk. The men said "What - tea with milk - you are offending us! It is only pregnant women who drink tea with milk!" So it was a bad impression on us, even though we had been given a good welcome.

I went to work for Mr. Braddick at Heazles. I did all sorts of work, from mucking out the cows to field work with cabbages. Italian prisoners of war worked with me. I loved them as they were

Later in the war, prisoners-of-war came to work on the farms. They brought their food with them and the farmers gave them drinks. They are remembered as good workers living in a camp in the woods by the A38 by Mountstephen Farm opposite the Bridwell turning.

so kind. They were always singing at the top of their voices as they worked. Mrs. Braddick had to warm up coffee for the prisoners - but she never gave me any. The Italians threatened to strike unless I was included in the hot drink. I got it! I didn't like the German P.O.W. I refused to work with him as he got fresh with me. He tried to get me to repeat German words to him - I didn't know what these words meant so I wouldn't do it.

The Royal Engineers were billeted in private houses and various other buildings in the village at the start of the war. The Quartermaster's store was at the rear of the Vicarage and the old National School was the cookhouse. The soldiers would sit outside on the wall in fine weather to eat their food. They were very popular and made to feel very welcome and when they eventually left, a lot of villagers went to the station to see them off.

A barrage balloon from Bristol was seen approaching Hemyock from the Culmbridge end, flying very low dragging a cable. Percy Pike, Harry Hold and Harry Bale decided to follow it and try to catch hold of it. They managed to get hold of it by the Rectory and tie it to the hedge. These men felt that they ought to be rewarded for their good deed, so Mrs Pike wrote a letter to the Air Ministry explaining what had happened, and asked a local policeman to sign it. She received a letter back acknowledging the event. About 6 months later, she sent the Air Ministry a reminder and this time three letters arrived, each containing a £1 reward. Each man gave Mrs Pike 2/6 making 7/6 for sending the letters to the Air Ministry.

A few bombs were dropped around this area during the second world war, two bombs at Symonsburrow, two at Mackam, and one came down at Fivebridges near the river. American airmen seemed to be everywhere, at Dunkeswell, Smeatharpe, and at Trickey Warren. At a dance one night at Hemyock two Americans came in, one toting a gun, looking for some offender. The incident certainly frightened the dancers for a while. There was a coloured American stationed at Smeatharpe, who they called Peewee. He was always giving the children sweets.

During the darkest days during the last war, we were woken up at 3a.m. with a huge bang. Thinking it was a bomb, we ran downstairs and found it to be a shell from guns from Taunton. Instead of hitting a German plane it exploded in the road outside my home in Station Road and blew hundreds of holes through our wooden double doors and right through our shed roof, and left quite a pit where it blew out the stones from the road.

Before her marriage, Betty worked first at Hemyock Place as a live-in maid for £1 a month. During the war she worked first in the canteen for Wimpy up at Dunkeswell where they were building the airfield for the US Naval Air force. The money was good and later she moved up to the canteen in Smeatharpe where the American Red Cross was based and had a hospital. She left there after V.J. Day and went to work in the milk factory. The runways were built with the help of gangs of women who came from Exeter and did all the labouring jobs including mixing cement and marking out the runways. They saw C47s, Dakotas and gliders go from there.

Memories of Men Who Did Not Return at the End of the War

Christopher and Michael Huth were the two youngest of five sons of Dr Huth. Christopher was the youngest, he was a musician and had a band. He joined the Royal Navy as an Ordinary Seaman and was commissioned. He was serving on a corvette when he was lost at sea. Michael was to be a barrister, but the war started and he joined the army. He was awarded the Military Medal before being commissioned in the Royal Tank Regiment. He was serving in Sicily when he was killed by an armour-piercing anti-tank shell and was buried by a fellow officer. Mrs. Huth was always so proud of her sons when they came home on leave and she would walk with them through the village. She died soon after the war, it was thought by many, of a broken heart.

Reginald Pike came from a large family and was brought up at Myrtle Cottage on Hillmoor. His

One of the Americans trained as a Dentist. Christmas cards were always exchanged and he returned with his wife to Clayhidon on two occasions.

83

father was a postman and carpenter, and his brother Fred was well known as a cattle dealer. Reg worked at Jerwoods, then for some time in a London hotel, and as a stoker on steam lorries before joining the Royal Navy. Several recall that it was obvious on his last leave that he had already faced considerable action. He was lost at sea early in the war in one of the large battleships.

John Fouracre was brought up with his brother and sister by their aunt, Mrs. Waygood. John loved the sea and served in the Maritime Royal Artillery - ack-ack - on board merchant ships. He sailed on the Empire Comet from a convoy assembly point in Canada bound for Liverpool. He was reported missing at sea. Mrs. Waygood said that she would never lock her front door again as she was sure he would come home.

Gwilym Whitcombe is buried in the only war grave in Culmstock cemetery; he died at the age of 24. He was always very bright at school and is well remembered by the girls as 'tall, dark and handsome'. He was good at sport, particularly football. On leaving school, his first job was collecting eggs for Wides of Hemyock and then he went on to be stoker to Bob Rowland on one of Scotts of Bampton's steam lorries. He took to service life and loved flying, becoming a Wireless Operator/Air Gunner in Lancasters serving with the 617 Squadron, the famous Dam Busters. On the day before V.J. Day, he was in a Wellington Bomber flying mail to Ireland. The plane crashed near Wellington in Shropshire. Gwilym had been made up to Warrant Officer the previous day. Dennis, his brother (who still lives in Culmstock), was in the army and a patient in the Military Hospital in Aldershot. When he heard of Gwilym's death he discharged himself from hospital, caught a train to Taunton and walked home from there, arriving in the early hours of the morning. Gwilym's flag covered coffin was brought home to Culmstock on the train. As the rest of the country celebrated V.J. Day, the Whitcombe family, relatives, friends and the whole village wept for Gwilym who had lived life to the full and died so tragically. "It was the biggest funeral the village has ever seen, the church was packed and as the first cars pulled up at the church the others were still leaving the other end of the village".

Welcome Home

The people of Culmstock collected money and had money raising events to give a welcome home party to the servicemen. The servicemen were all presented with a certificate and £5. Jimmy Collier gave a large part of Hillmoor Common to the parish and plans were drawn up for a playing field with cricket and football pitches, tennis courts and a pavilion. Extensive drainage was carried out and when it was almost complete it was realised that the cost of maintenance for the ambitious scheme would be exorbitant. A meeting was called in the village hall and when villagers realised that a charge on the rates would be inevitable it was voted that the project be abandoned. The remaining funds were used to plant two copper beeches at Hunters Way and outside the village hall. For 40 years the village land at Hillmoor was abandoned, the trees grew, plants and wild life flourished. In recent years the land has been transformed into a nature reserve with stiles for access. The school children have visited the site and now a leaflet is available incorporating the children's art work and writings. A happy ending to the story of the Welcome Home Fund for ex-servicemen, many of them now grandfathers.

❖ ❖ ❖

Don't Wish Your Life Away

I was not born in the Blackdowns, but my family moved to Somerset/Devon in 1937. My father suffered with a bad chest, and the air in Derbyshire where we had a smallholding/chicken farm was polluted. The doctor advised my father to move the family to an area with clean air. This is how I arrived as a small child, with my mother, father and older brother in a Churchstanton Farmhouse, which is still there, called Clivehayes. My father bought the smallholding from a Mr. Blackmore (a member of the Lorna Doone R.D. Blackmore family). All water had to be pumped from a well by hand. We cooked by paraffin stove - and our home was lit by candles and oil lamps. The farmhouse had a thatched roof, and at one time had been a brewery.

There was little need to shop as everything was made at home. We grew most of our own food, had our own milk and eggs. What couldn't be provided was ordered from the grocer who called once a fortnight, and he took the order for the next delivery.

We rode in our pony and trap, walked or bicycled along narrow, empty lanes as there was no motor transport. On the rare visits we made to Taunton we went in the pony and trap to Churchinford, and parked it in the stables behind the post office, before catching the bus. We went to Churchstanton Church and sat in the boxed pews so I could not see over the top of the wooden partition.

I can remember the day war was declared. I was so excited. My mother, however, burst into tears. "Your brother and your father will be taken to fight, and will both be killed" she sobbed. I couldn't understand it - but I remember her tears.

Our peaceful lives were soon to be shattered. The first area to be taken over was Trickey Warren (by Culmhead Radio Station). This was the base for the Polish and Czech Air Force. Their whole lives were geared towards personal revenge for the destruction of their families and countries, and when the German planes came over the Blackdowns on their way to bomb Bristol and Cardiff, they attacked the German planes with no thought for their own survival.

A hutted camp for American Infantry was built at Stapley. The majority of the troops were black. My mother had always threatened my brother and me when we were naughty with - "If you don't behave the black man will get you!" My terror was great, as it wasn't just one black man who would get me, it was hundreds! When we got used to them we found them delightful and very kind to children.

Smeatharpe Airfield was built and local farmers could earn £50 a day (an enormous sum in those times) moving earth with their horse and carts. In order to cash in on this source of wealth, my father bought a cart horse called Captain. Captain proved a bad investment! My brother couldn't manage him. He said Captain had too many feet and no brakes so the horse didn't earn his keep. He joined the animals on our smallholding - forty pigs, five cows and many head of chicken.

The airfield was occupied by American personnel. Our lanes were filled with army transport and marching soldiers. The noise from the American Troops housed in corrugated iron huts, particularly at meal times, could be heard clearly from our farm. One day two American officers leaned over our gate and asked if they could see over our farm as they had never seen a smallholding. My father showed them everything and they were intrigued by the inglenook fireplace, and the bread oven. After they departed we found that they had left a box of chocolate bars for us. The Americans were a generous people - and very homesick. My brother brought home a young 19 year old American service man called Jack Lagar one Christmas Eve. My mother was decorating the Christmas tree, and he cried when he saw it. He was just missing his own family at Christmas so much. Jack survived the war and kept in touch when he returned to America. Many lasting friendships were made during this time, and each year Americans come to Dunkeswell for a reunion. It was from here that President Kennedy's brother flew to his death. The Kennedy family came to Dunkeswell for the blessing of the organ given to Dunkeswell Church in his memory. Our farm was very close to the airfield. We had landing lights in our farm yard, and as the Liberators took off and landed our house shook. I used to wave to the pilots with a Union Jack as they took off and landed. I was waving my flag one day when to my horror I saw the German markings on the wings of a plane very, very low. The German pilot waved back to

me. He could easily have shot me - but he just waved. He must have been on a reconnaissance flight and could easily have machine gunned me, but he didn't harm a little girl just waved.

At night, Smeatharpe was lit by search lights, but father still hid his storm lantern under his heavy coat when he visited the animals at night. Our farm was a dangerous place to be during a raid. My father built us a shelter in a dug out hole in the bank down the lane and covered it with sandbags. My father had whisky to keep out the cold and we had water - but we survived even though it was often bitterly cold and damp. We were all issued with gas masks, which we had to carry with us at all times. Mine never fitted very well. I was too big for the Mickey Mouse type issued for very small children, and had a standard one. If one laughed in a gas mask the window steamed up, and you couldn't see out. It was very claustrophobic and smelt of rubber. We were told that if gas was dropped by the Germans, Mr. Pitman the air raid warden would get on his bicycle and ride as fast as he could round the lanes, blowing a whistle and whirling a wooden rattle. One day my mother thought she heard Mr. Pitman's whistle, so we spent the day in our gas masks - a horrible experience.

American officers came regularly to talk to us children at school. We received detailed instructions and warnings about touching or picking up unexploded bombs and bullets and how we should behave when the Germans machine gunned the airfields. We had to lie on our tummies and put our hands over our heads. One night a German plane crashed near our school playground. Four of the crew were killed, and we were shown the outline of their bodies that had been burnt into the ground. They were like four cut out gingerbread men. One had escaped from the burning wreckage. He had lost part of his hand and walked some way in the blackout trying to find a farmhouse. When he eventually found one the farmer came to the door with a gun. The German was convinced that his last moment had come because they had been told that if they baled out over England the locals would shoot them on sight. The four remains of the German crew were buried with full military honours in Upottery Church Yard.

The Americans were very kind to children. On the way back from school I passed the sentry box guarding the entrance to the airfield. The American Military Policemen became my friends and they always had an orange or some sweets for me. They called me "their lovely little Limey". By our standards the Americans were very rich - with access to food and goods which even in peacetime were unobtainable for us - but they tried to share. On Thanksgiving Days I remember they had a party for us. Piles of food, turkey, gravy and vegetables, and bags full of something rather like rock, which they poured onto our place settings. I can remember some of it fell sometimes into the gravy, but it was still sweet. We also had paper hats.

The leftovers from their food was given to a man called Sam Wool. He collected the swill for his pigs and cooked it up in cauldrons in the lane. This resulted in an infestation of rats which swarmed everywhere. I can remember riding my bicycle home from school and having to lift my legs onto the handlebars to avoid them.

Distribution of food, via Ration Books, was brilliant. I can never remember being really hungry - but I never felt really full. We were lucky, I expect, living on a farm. My father set up snares to catch rabbits and I used to hear the poor little creatures scream when they were trapped. We ate a great many rabbits as they made a tasty, free meal. Not so delicious was whale meat - obtainable off ration- but edible. I don't remember eating any of our own chickens because we could get good money for them, also all our eggs were collected by the egg packing station. After school my job was to collect them in buckets and wash each one by hand.

I attended the Lady Sidmouth C. of E. School in Smeatharpe (now a private house). I walked to school, later bicycled, in all weathers. This was a happy place, never more than thirty children, even when the few evacuees came. At the front of the main classroom was a wooden panel. On Sundays this panel was opened to reveal an altar - and served as Smeatharpe Parish Church. During the war all the school windows were latticed into diamond shapes with sticky tape to prevent the shattered glass falling on us. When I went to Secondary School in Honiton, I left my bicycle for safety behind the sentry box before picking up the school bus.

On Saturday evenings, as I got older, I was allowed to go to Churchinford Village Hall for the "Social Evening". The hall was lit by gas, and I can recall the woman who ran the Socials climbing the ladder to light the gas mantles. We danced to a piano, played games, and there were often

There were no ingredients to make Shapes (blancmange), but my mother made a good substitute by boiling up five laurel leaves in one pint of milk. This set well and was a pretty green colour. One thing I really longed for was a banana as I could remember what it was like to have one before rationing.

90

sandwiches. The great attraction, of course, was the American men who came crowding in and joined in everything. We had so much fun.

By this time my father had a small car. Even for farmers petrol was severely rationed, but we used to pile into it for trips to Taunton Market. We parked the car behind the George Hotel in High Street for 6d a day. We would stop for petrol at Trull Garage. The petrol was called National Benzol, and was pumped up by hand by the attendant. You could see the petrol in the glass cylinder - eleven pence ha'penny a gallon, I remember. One day a tow truck full of whistling Americans cut the corner too closely, and pulled off our mud guard. My father ran into the road in anger, but couldn't catch them. We were without a mud guard until well after the end of the war because no replacement was available.

Taunton would be unrecognisable to today's teenagers. The Parade was covered with enormous water tanks as precaution against fire bombs. In my favourite shop, Woolworth's, many of the counters were covered with sheets of brown paper because there were no goods to sell. If word got around that they had a consignment of shampoo, face cream, or, even more sought after, kirby grips, a queue would quickly form. All shops closed on one afternoon a week and, of course, on Sunday.

There was a large feeding centre (called a British Restaurant) above Dixons. You could get a cheap meal there, exchanging money for coloured tokens.

D.Day Preparations

Our first indication of something happening was on our way to Taunton Market, seeing tents erected all along the sides of the road in Culmhead area. As we slowed down to look, we heard a voice shouting "Aunty Clara!" and a young soldier coming towards us. To our amazement it was my mother's nephew from Derbyshire. He was not allowed to speak to us.

Soon after this episode we were not allowed to go out or go to school for three weeks. The roads were blocked solid with troops and lorries, as they assembled for the D. Day landings. Suddenly the camps were deserted. The hills were silent for the first time in many years. It was an eerie silence. We had landed in France.

When I left school, my friend cycled over and told me that they were looking for six young ladies to staff the Forces Canteen at Dunkeswell. I went with her for an interview, and to my delight got the job. The Canteen was run by the Salvation Army. I lived in, but the Salvation Army carefully chaperoned us. We were not allowed to go out unaccompanied, and even a visit to the Camp Cinema was only allowed if accompanied. I longed to be 21 and free - but my mother always said to me - "Don't wish your life away". I have always remembered this, particularly in bad times, and have tried to follow her wise advice as she urged me to do and I have - "Not wished my life away".

❖ ❖ ❖

Dunkeswell Days

Dunkeswell has been my life. Mother, the youngest of 11 children, was born and brought up in Garden Cottage which was purchased by my Grandfather and Uncle from the Simcoe Estate in 1923 at the grand price of £125.

My father came to Dunkeswell as a small boy. He was the first man in Dunkeswell to own a motor cycle. Bill Lane from the Forge was the second. I remember my father telling how Bill Lane overtook him on Wingate Hill shouting as he passed "Where have you been Clar? (his name being Clarence), Bird nesting?" Needless to say a couple of miles on there was Bill Lane up in the hedge, bike and all.

My father started work as a well digger and told many stories. One well in particular was at Blackdown Garth, I believe Mr. & Mrs. Brian Jeans are still using the same well. My parents were married on Bampton Fair Day 1930, and went to Corner House at Luppitt for a short time where I was born in 1931. Then we moved to a brand new council house in Awliscombe. Father had priority for tenancy as he was now a thatcher classed as Agricultural Worker.

News came that Mr. King, who was the landlord of the Royal Oak, wanted to leave, so being Dunkeswell people my parents wanted to move back. At Christmas 1937 back we came. What an adventure. My brother and myself couldn't believe the space and so many doors to go through.

Then we found Mrs. Wynn's sweet shop where we could buy Sherbert Dabs for one penny, and Aniseed Balls, Traffic Lights and Bluebird Toffees eight for 1d. We went to Mrs. Stevens in the evening for scalded milk that was about a $1^{1}/_{2}$d a pint. I particularly remember the milk because it was winter and the roads were slippery with ice and I fell down and wasted the milk. Boy! Did I get into trouble and it really wasn't my fault.

Mr. Stamp from Weston used to come around selling ice cream, he had a 3 wheeled tricycle. Cornets were $\frac{1}{2}$d each.

When I was twelve years old, I got diphtheria, but I survived. Dr.Griffin's father saved my life. That epidemic was quite something, the school was closed down for a while. Luckily mother paid into the Hospital Aid Society, so when the bill came for my stay in Whipton Hospital for three weeks, the Hospital Aid Society paid up all £12.

All Kinds of Weather

The Great Blizzard of 1962-63

As I am one of the older generation, I thought the younger ones might be interested in our experiences of that severe winter. The blizzard, or rather blizzards, as it was repeated many times, from December 1962 - February 1963, started on Boxing Day of 1962 and continued until the end of February 1963. It would snow all day and block roads and railway lines and cause tremendous chaos. When it stopped snowing, it did not melt because of bitter temperatures and force 9 gales from the east. If we cleared a path one day, the wind drifted the snow and we had to do it again next day, some drifts up to twenty feet high. The roads were full and we walked on top of the hedges. The only ones to enjoy it were the children, who were off school for 6 to 8 weeks. Our biggest problem was the milk, as this was a dairy farm. The milk lorry did not get to us to collect the milk from the end of December until the first of March. So the farmers had to load up the churns, and take them to Hemyock factory. The tractors could manage the roads, but no lorries or cars. The milk from the farm was often put down the drain when it was impossible to get down to St Ivel in Hemyock even with the tractor.

At that time we normally had all requirements brought to our door, but with the roads so bad, no one could get to us. When the milk had been delivered to the factory, we filled the empty churns with meat, bread and groceries, and it was delivered around to all our neighbours. After a few weeks some of the neighbours plucked up courage and rode on the tractor and trailer with us. One householder made his own transport, with three or four sledges joined together and pulled by a lawn mower, to get his provisions.

The wind and frost were so severe, that the frost penetrated two feet into the ground. A water main pipe at Cove, near Tiverton, was completely frozen, and they had to lay a polythene pipe across the snow to keep up the supply. The main pipe remained frozen until June!

The river Exe was frozen over at Tiverton, providing much enjoyment for the skaters. The average temperature for January was 28.9 degrees, and it was said to be the coldest January for 150 years. At Colyford, the ice on the river was a foot thick and explosives were used to break it up. Our telephone wires all came down, and a cable was laid across the snow to keep up the service.

The ewes had to be kept in the farmyard for six weeks, and it wasn't until March that a lorry containing cattle food was able to get to us. The conditions suffered by those of us who had to struggle to feed the cattle in the fields were unbelievably awful. Sheep had to be dug out of drifts, sometimes only using gloved hands in order not to harm them.

In spite of frozen pipes, life inside the farmhouse continued as normal as we had always been really self sufficient. I always did a large shop for dry ingredients before Christmas, so we were well prepared for the siege. We made our own butter and cream, we had our own poultry and eggs, meat from our own animals and wood from our own land. We survived the worst that the severe weather could do to us, until the wonderful relief of Spring.

To Work by Tractor

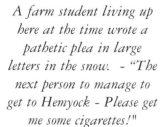

A farm student living up here at the time wrote a pathetic plea in large letters in the snow. - "The next person to manage to get to Hemyock - Please get me some cigarettes!"

After a very heavy snowfall one night the next day was sunny and the snow melted slightly. My daughter worked in a bank in Wellington so she couldn't go to work. The Bank Manager rang up to say that they had a lot of work on and could she come to work. I said it was impossible as the roads were level to the hedge tops with snow and he said "Please try!". I had a small Allis Chalmer's B tractor, which was very light, and I managed to get to Wellington and home over the top! A neighbour asked me if I had been out with the tractor and I said "Yes". So he went out with his heavy tractor but got really stuck, only recovering it in early March when the snow finally melted.

The Cloud Burst July 5th 1963

On Thursday July 5th 1963, Hemyock suffered the results of a cloudburst. Haymaking had been in progress and the loose hay had been washed from the fields so a build up occurred up at Green Lane, with hay being pushed against the hedges. Then the hedges gave way, and down came the water.

The church was flooded, the coconut matting was soaked and later had to be hung out over the church walls to dry. Mrs. Pike remembers it was a Thursday as she was at Country Dancing, and Michael, who was at Scouts, had put his bike in the porch. The water was half way up the wheels when he came out, and a car parked in a shed in the saw yard was afloat. The Castle Park field was flooded as the pile of stones up at the church end directed the cloudburst into a flood.

The Great Flood July 10th 1967

We were lucky to be hill people as those living in the lower lying areas of Culmstock and Hemyock suffered badly. It was about half past five to six when we heard the first clap of thunder. Soon the thunder and lightning were continuous and the heavens opened. There were no raindrops, just solid water cascading down. We put on macs and wellies and braved out to move some sows we were afraid might drown.

The worst of the flood water poured off our land into the valley. However, during one of the worst storms, my eighteen month old daughter was asleep in her pram in the passage leading to the dairy.

Water rushed through the back door and completely submerged the wheels of the pram. A cardboard box nesting our kittens was on the floor by the pram and the rushing floodwater drowned them. We were able to disperse the water by pushing it out through the front door.

In minutes we were soaked to the skin, the lightning was playing on the metal gates and the thunder seemed all around us, the water raced down through the farm in a torrent. I was terrified. It just went on and on. Eventually we were driven indoors; there was nothing more we could do. When the rain eventually eased we went down to look at the stream, which had turned into a vast river. We wondered whether to ring friends at Culmstock to warn them, but by then we had no telephone or electric.

The weather from mid-May had been poor, it wasn't the quantity of rain, just that it never seemed to leave off for long, the grass was never dry.

We went, as a family, down to Tiverton Grammar School for a concert, just as the rain started. By the 9 p.m. interval the beating on the roof of the Hall was deafening so we decided to stay no longer. In Sampford Peverell, the car came to a halt. Enough water had splashed up to drench the distributor. A mopping up operation under the bonnet got it started while standing in the pouring rain.

In the gathering gloom at Whitehall a neighbour flagged us down with a hand torch. Could we help rescue a sow? The flood water from the river was hallway up the slope to the level crossing, and on a piece of dry ground behind the mill below Whitehall Halt stood a sow trapped between the flood water and the now raging mill leat. To have attempted to cross the leat would have been suicidal, but the sow looked safe enough if it stayed put.

Meantime, in the valley bottom, trouble was brewing. Much mown grass was still lying on the hay fields beside the river, and this grass was now being swept down by the flood waters to catch up in the cross fences. These then formed impenetrable breakwaters. When they were no longer able to take the strain, the fences gave way to release a huge surge of water down to the next fence. About the time that we were viewing the sow my friend at Westown went down to the river to see how his young cattle were faring. He could just make them out, marooned on a knoll in the middle of the flood water. As he watched, one of the surges lifted them all off their feet and amid much bellowing, swept them down the river to Culmstock.

Next morning there wasn't a cloud in the sky! A perfect English summer's day. The storm seemed like a bad dream. After milking we went to Westown to help look for the young stock. The flood water had greatly subsided and we were able to follow the river to Culmstock. We soon came upon a dead heifer and fearing the worst, we pressed on only to find the fields bereft of stock. Then at Culmstock, a miracle! The river at Culmstock flows tight beside the road and abruptly turns left to pass under the bridge. Cattle and sheep borne down by the flood had been saved from being carried under the bridge. Instead they had been deposited on the large meadow beside the railway station. When we arrived, the field was a seething mass of animals with the farmers busily trying to identify and separate out their own stock. No more fatalities for Westown, though one or two whose legs had been entangled in barbed wire subsequently developed gangrenous wounds. With relief, and in delightful sunshine, we drove the young cattle home.

We had lived in Culmstock for just one week and had been busy decorating all day. Bill went up to have a bath, he looked out of the bedroom window and saw vehicle headlights reflecting in water. Bill shouted downstairs "Can we see the river from here?" and I replied "No, of course not, it's too low". "In that case" said Bill, "I think the river has flooded". We went to investigate, the water had reached Harts Row and Henry Berry's cottage.

Culm Valley Inn

The water came in so quickly there was nothing we could do about it but, not to be deterred, Robby was still pulling pints for the customers standing up to their knees in water. The water was half way up the stairs and a heavy door floated off its hinges and hit me on the head. The piano was floating around, and the freezers which contained the food for a wedding had tipped over and were afloat. The river was like a wall of water as it had changed its course and went straight down the valley.

Next day I saw that the clothes I had been wearing were stained to the armpits. Harry Alford spent all next day hosing down trying to get rid of the mud and sludge. My china cupboard was thick with mud and in a cupboard that had borne the full force of the water I remember the tins of fruit had all been knocked together so much that they were like a pulp. Everything in our safe was ruined, but funnily enough the electricity never went off.

At Fisher's the Butchers

The water rushed through the house and yard. Bill went out to see what he could save in the barn. As the water rushed through, it closed the door and he was trapped, he thought he would drown. The water receded when it reached his shoulders, it was at its highest at 10.20p.m. The force of the water burst the garage doors open and the van went down the river. We didn't find it for more than a week, the water was still so muddy we still couldn't see it but eventually we found it beyond the fisherman's bridge. It had obviously gone down on its side as it was battered about, but amazingly none of the glass was broken, neither were the headlights. The morning after the flood, David caught a trout in the kitchen!

Berry's Garage

Over a dozen vehicles were swamped by the flood and many of them were write-offs. Three cars were on the forecourt; the water moved them around and jammed them together. Next day all they could do was serve a little petrol and try to clear the place up. The damage ran into thousands of pounds.

Strawbridge's Store

We were having supper when the vicar knocked on the door to tell us there was a flood warning but we didn't take much notice as we had never been flooded. When we had finished our meal I looked out of the shop door and saw that the white lines down the middle of the road were disappearing. I rushed in to tell Basil "I think we're in for it this time".

The water came up so fast we had to rush and do what we could. We went out to move the boxes of soap powder in the garage, we had taken a large delivery of biscuits that day and we hurriedly took them upstairs, but there wasn't time to save much. The shop doors began to move as they took the force of the water. Basil found something to shore it up or it would have been a lot worse. The van outside began to float and Basil waded out and saved it by tying it to the gatepost of Fisher's field.

Next day we found that the Triumph had knocked out the side of the wooden garage as it had been buffeted around. It was the only day ever that we hadn't opened the shop. Lily Clyst came down and scrubbed round the shop all day trying to get rid of the stinking mud. We had a television set brought back that day, and I remember the T.V. man squelching across the sitting room carpet. There was water in the paraffin and the deep freeze contents were ruined.

It was some time after half past nine when the water suddenly rose, it came to the level of

Strawbridges' window and our bottom step. Teddy Cavill went off to get us a sandbag to put at our front door, but the water started to recede just in time for us. We looked out of the back door and all the empty Calor Gas cylinders were bobbing around like corks. As the water started to go down we went next door to give what help we could. I can still see the dried fruit, loose in those days, disappearing in the gushing water as we threw it out of the front door.

One of Ten

I was one of ten children and and we used to make our own fun, we were happy as larks. Until I was twelve we lived at Red Ball, then in 1930 we moved to Woodgate into a 100 ft. wooden army hut. There was a long corridor from one end to the other, five bedrooms, a kitchen and a parlour. In the parlour was a beautiful inlaid rosewood grand piano with ivory keys; it was dated 1808, Broadwood, London. It had belonged to my great grandfather who was blind and played by ear. None of us could play, we were not interested, so my father gave it to the Horniman Museum in London.

My father had traction engines, a Burrell steam roller and saw benches. He would haul flints from the quarries up by Culmstock Beacon for making up the roads. They would throw the clinkers in as well and roll them down.

There was no water in the house and so we got the water for washing from a stream up across a field. The drinking water we fetched in two buckets twice a day from Scots Shute (a half mile round trip). We went up the lanes to get it and then we

would stop and have a chat with the Squires and the Quicks. We grew all our own vegetables and mother made boiled roly poly suet puddings, which were delicious, and beautiful rabbit stew. Dudley Lewis delivered groceries from Wellington in a motor bike and sidecar. When we moved into Hunters Way in 1948 we thought it was heaven. For the first time we didn't have to collect our water but just turn the tap, and of course we hadn't had electricity before.

When I left school I went out doing housework, polishing ranges and grates with Zebo polish, scrubbing floors and cleaning carpets with a dustpan and brush. I worked for one family for 49 years, I also worked at the Culm Valley Inn and Hemyock factory for twenty four and a half years, I always cycled there.

❖ ❖ ❖

Fun and Games

Tennis

I left school at 15 years of age and started playing tennis in the summer of 1930. There were two grass courts at that time and I can well remember the men players conveying the large heavy roller from the Bowls Club, heaving it up the road and rolling the two grass courts before a tennis match was played. We had the tea intervals in the Bowls Club shed with the North side open to the elements of the weather, wet or fine!

A hard court was fixed up after members' gifts of money and various fund raising events but it is now the public children's playground. I was treasurer of the Club when the Second World War broke out. Most of the players left for various war services - consequently the Club was closed. The money I held for the Club was passed on to the local Social Services to be earmarked for the possibility of the tennis club reopening after the war.

The war ended and a small group of past members tried to get the club started again, but through lack of support it did not materialise. Now a new generation of young players has reopened it with their two new hard courts.

Hemyock Bowling Club

The Club was formed in 1905 and my Grandfather, Edward Lutley, was among the first members. My mother was one of the first ladies to form the Ladies Section of the Club. It was in 1964 I decided to 'have a go' at the game of bowls. I have memories of various competitions arranged over the years with the 17 trophies I won. It was in 1996 that 'we girls' won the Mid Devon Ladies League for the first time - we won it again in 1997!

The legendary three times World Champion bowler, David Bryant, visited our Club in 1967 to open our new kitchen. He visited us the second time to open our new 'proper' pavilion. I have his signature written on the programme of the match we played with him on 16th July 1988. We were very honoured to have such a very important and famous Bowls player showing off his skills on our Green! He once said that "Bowls is a game for young players as well as old players!" - so say all of us!!

Dissent Among the Bowlers!

"Wyndham",
Hemyock.
Aug. 9th, 1933.

Dear Sir,

An urgent Meeting of the Committee, of which you are a Member, will take place in the Club Pavilion tomorrow, Thursday night at 7p.m.

AGENDA

To adjudicate on a brawl alleged to have taken place on the Green on Tuesday evening, between Messrs. F. Melhuish and R.A.H.. Strawbridge, as a result of which the Treasurer has resigned his Office and Membership.

I am suggesting to the parties concerned that they should not be represented at the Meeting other than by written statements of their position. I consider it is very important that the Committee should deal with the matter as soon as possible, in view of Saturday's match, and I may say that if you consider the Pavilion an unsuitable place to meet, my house is available for the purpose at the time stated.

Yours faithfully,
Hon. Secretary.
Howard L. Wide

Culmstock Cricket Club 1947-1960

There was a very strong Cricket Club in the village around the 1900's. I have a photo of a stylish clubhouse, cricketers in elegant whites and chic caps surrounded by fashionable ladies. The club that was formed in 1947 couldn't have been more different, as most of the founders had returned from active service in the war, village life was quiet, we were all a little wild and missed the comradeship of service life. A cricket club would seem to be the answer, we would be able to play a game and release some of our energy, have some fun and indulge in a few celebrations with our friends.

The qualification for enrolment was simple: you were a good sport, good humoured, companionable, could drink a pint or two, and were not under petticoat government. Dress requirements could be described as optional, a white or nearly white shirt, trousers, grey, but not the demob variety. White shirts and flannels began to appear later, most of which seemed to be resurrected from the 1900's era. A fixture list was soon put together with neighbouring villages, with similar ideas and approved ways of playing the game. Holding an inquest in the local after the game was a must, and when playing away you stayed as guest of the opposing team until the landlord called time.

Drink driving laws were not in existence and many after match stories can be told, becoming a little embellished as time goes on. The most notable of these is the following one and is perfectly true.

After an evening game at Holcombe Rogus, we decided to get a pint in at the Red Ball on the way home. John Knowlman was leading with half the team, closely followed by me with the other half. On rounding a bend we came upon the local constable on his bike, he was not in danger but prompted by his instinct for survival mounted the grass verge and disappeared into the ditch. John pressed on and it was immediately apparent that it was prudent for me to do the same. We were relieved to hear nothing more of the incident and he would have been surprised to learn that his embarrassing demise was caused by a respected local auctioneer and his accomplice the son of a local magistrate!

Many characters were part of the team. There was Jimmy Collier our lord of the manor, a small chap with a big personality and great fun at the pub piano; Freddy Alford, a most generous man who specialised in liquid lunches; Cecil Pym, his ample figure restricting his fielding; Dennis Hoile, a solid character and solid cricketer; Bernard Thorne, whose claim to fame was hitting five sixes in one over; Buster Bull, who kept his entire wardrobe in no particular order in the back of his Austin 7. We missed him during a game at Churchinford and found him in the long grass beyond the boundary having a quiet smoke.

We soon found a permanent ground on the Uffculme road at Pilemoor. Home game teas were provided by the Thorne family in the kitchen at the Old Bakery on a large table to seat over twenty, doughnuts, chudleys and cream, etc. Wonderful!! We would then trek back to the field and try to play the rest of the game. On Sunday mornings we would all gather at the ground and make repairs. At 12 o'clock prompt, return to Ilminster for a quick one before lunch.

We formed a skittle team and played league skittles during the winter. Such was the gregarious nature of our members we never hung up our boots or mugs the whole year round. As soon as the club was formed, we were instantly supported by the community and we tried to respond by having a dinner every year to entertain them and they to entertain us. Local dignitaries on some occasions have been known to let their hair down. One professional gentleman I recall told stories that would have made the legendary Max Miller blush.

Fifty years on, the club is still going strong, thanks to many people who kept it going for many years, the redoubtable Betty Symons and family come to mind. I often wonder in spite of better facilities, kit, etc., whether the present members enjoy the club as much as we did? I doubt it!!

Hemyock Cricket Club

This was set up in 1895 by Rev. Stamp who obtained permission from a Mr Goddard of the Social Services committee to allow the game to be played on what is now the Recreation Field. It lapsed a couple of times and was re-started in 1953 and again in 1985.

Girl Guides

Miss Lowry came down with her mother and father from London and they built a new house over the Culmstock road, Woodridings. She was secretary to the manager at the factory. After a while she decided to start a Girl Guide company in the village, about twenty turned up. We were sorted out into Patrols, I was leader of Daisy Patrol, it was just like being in the army. When we had our uniform we had brimmed navy blue felt hats which we had to iron with a damp cloth to keep them flat, starch our triangular ties and fold them correctly, polish our badges with Brasso, also polish our shoes. First thing she did at the beginning of each meeting was to line us up for inspection. We tied knots, played games and did competitions. In the summer we used to go up to Sandpits and Conigar.

One week she told us to take a tin with a wire handle, filled with water, and an egg. Off we went up to Conigar. It took us quite a time to cut the turf and to collect some kindling and a few larger pieces of wood to keep the fire going once lit. My Patrol did well, got a good fire going, placed our tins on the fire to boil our eggs. We got the egg cups and the bread and butter ready, put on the billycan to make some tea and just as we were going to take our eggs out there was an explosion and my egg had blown out the tin into the bracken. Miss Lowry was furious and said I did not set a good example to the younger guides. I used a Golden Syrup tin and put the wire around the tin to make a handle. Everyone else had bored holes and made a handle. In the end I told Miss Lowry I didn't like boiled eggs anyway. The next time we went cooking we had a fry up, black specks all over our eggs, bacon and fried bread, but it all added to the flavour. We mixed flour and water to a dough, wound it round a piece of stick, called it a damper and when cooked, filled it with jam. We did have some fun and are still living to tell the tale.

Rangers

When we were too old for Guides a Ranger Patrol was formed; we helped the Guides and then we had an hour and a half at the Old Rectory, the home of Mrs. Leckye. We had one of the back rooms to keep our equipment and have our meeting each week. Her daughter Jill was a Ranger and about half a dozen others. We took an interest in local affairs, did a First Aid course, studied the history of the village, and even cycled to Sheldon to the Waterworks and had a guided tour. We often went to the sand pits and did a bit of stalking, and we even pitched a tent one night, lit a fire and entertained the Rector, Mr. Ketchley, and some visiting clergy to the parish.

In 1947 we were invited to join the Exmouth Sea Rangers for a holiday in France. The cost was £20 for the fortnight. We had a wonderful time, but we were not very good at rowing a boat. I took over from Miss Ivy Wide and ran the Brownie Pack for over twenty years, and when I resigned Janice Fuller took over the Pack.

In 1951 a goodwill message Girl Guide gesture was taken on foot, by bicycle and on horseback, taking a month. Devon Girl Guides carried a scroll bearing a message of friendship from the West Country on its way to Oxford, where it was handed to the Egyptian delegate to the World Conference to the Guide movement. As far as possible the route was along bridle paths and pony tracks. After the Cullompton Guides and Brownies had left the scroll in the hands of Mrs. Quick at Sheldon, it was taken by the Hemyock group of Rangers, Guides and Brownies to the handover ceremony at Smeatharpe. A Somerset Ranger took the scroll on horseback into Somerset and across another county.

On St. George's Day we always had a parade at Tiverton. We looked forward to these outings to a different church each time, it was lovely to meet everyone.

Old Skip of Hemyock Scouts

Skip is remembered by many Scouts and their families for the unstinting contribution he made to the young people of the Blackdowns. Here are some of his reflections written in 1996 in his seventieth year.

Over the camp at Huish Woods will be drifts of wood smoke, in the drift will be memories for Skip and many others.

1972. The arrival, in Hemyock, of the Danes from Tønder, including a load of bearded Seniors/Ventures - the chaps had the beards, the young ladies were as beautiful as all Danish girls are. We camped together at Torbay, where we made history - it was the first time ever that boys and girls had camped together - can you believe it! Flemming Birkvad clasping a huge mallet led the visiting Cub Scouts, including Chris Pettigrew, now Akela, around the camp site.

1974. Our first visit to Denmark. We sailed on the lovely new 'Dana Regina'. It was a year when Danish Scouts and Guides joined together at the beautiful site above Lim-Fjorden. The excitement of a camp with 18,000 of us wearing different sub camp colours, forming the map of Denmark! We blew and burst 18,000 paper bags.

1977. A grand camp together in the mountains of Wales. Lis Hanson and her company of girls joined us and an amusing camp fire stunt about Skip worrying about litter! (He still does!).

1980. Stevninghus. What a camp! 7,000 knee deep in mud and later floating in water. A camp we would not have missed for anything.

1983. Fishponds sanctuary where the Royal Marines dropped in by parachute. What fun scouting is!

1986. The beautiful island of Fyn/Funen. Grand weather, a splendid programme, and a treasured visit to Copenhagen. At Fyn/Funen, an enormous Danebrog was seen gently flying below a bright blue sky. Memories!!

1988. Fishponds sanctuary in less than kind weather where some of us met the HRH Prince Edward.

1990. Bredeadal was a vintage camp in blazing sunshine with visits from dear friends, a programme brilliantly designed and food second to none. We went to Logun Kloster in bare feet and walked on the scorching pavements. By 1990 I had young leaders who did all the work! I was able to take things easy and each morning enjoyed a walk across the dikes to the church spire at Bredebro

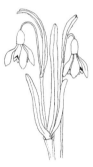

1992. I retired and had absolutely nothing to do except enjoy an outstandingly wonderful camp at Gutter Tor refuge on my beloved Dartmoor. A camp with a host of memories.

1994. Sadly I could not join the camp at Bla Sommer but was delighted to hear all about the excitement.

1996. Now in my seventieth year I was invited to join the camp at Huish Woods. It will add to my memories whilst you are busy creating yours. Importantly, I thank all those lovely families in Denmark and here, who have provided such wonderful hospitality. The friendship with you all means so much long may you continue.

Bless you all
Old Skip

Culmstock Scout Troop

The other day I turned out the log of the 1st Culmstock Scout Troop, and thumbing through the pages brought back such happy memories. I was 13 when the troop was formed in June 1935, and we were fitted for our uniforms by Extons of Wellington. They also provided us with a large Union Jack - it was later carried by the British contingent when we marched past the Chief Scout, Lord Baden-Powell at the jamboree at Mount Edgcumbe in August 1937. We were very proud.

Some of our first camp and fire lighting exercises were down by the river at the Hams - happy days. The spot where we camped is no longer there; the river has changed course and washed it away!

Pat McElwee was the Group Scout Master and Stephen Hamilton was the Assistant Scout Master. Toby Huth (Dr. Huth's son) and his wife were home from Australia where they were involved in Scouting, and they played a large part in the early days. On November 5th 1935, we had a bonfire and fireworks on Hillmoor, there was a large crowd and over 50 motor tyres were used for the fire. In 1936 we all wore black armbands to attend the memorial service for King George V.

Fire lighting was one of our main activities, I think these few excerpts from the log will give you an idea:-

March 14th. Fire lighting by river. A decided win for Otters (I was Patrol Leader!) The Hounds were badly organised in spite of the second going home to fetch shavings and paper (!!) they did not get theirs going till the Otters had boiled their dixie of tea.

March 28th. Fire lighting test by river by patrols. Otters were determined not to be beaten and were not. Otters - two men passed. Hounds - one P.L. Thorne gallantly rescued a football from the river and in so doing sat down in midstream. Result - a fine display of clothes drying at J. Earland's fire.

April 11th. Troop meeting at Beacon. Pikey and P. Earland passed fire lighting. They couldn't very well fail as there was a strong wind and plenty of dry stuff.

April 25th. Troop meeting poorly attended because of the broadcast of Cup Final.

July 5th-6th. Camp at Maidendown - the fire would not light. We gave it up as a bad job but a Girl Guide managed to do it after we had given up hope. Three cheers for the Girl Guides. The night was not very peaceful, a nightjar kept everybody awake for an hour. The general feeling is nightjars should not be allowed to exist.

Accidents were: -

(1)   Percy Parsons falling out of a tree. Result - breath knocked out of him.

(2)   G. McKiel came off his bike. Result - grazed elbow.

(3)   Bernard Thorne brought a bread saw. Result - Bordie cut himself.

(4)   Lewis burnt his leg on A.S.M.'s Rudge (motorbike).

There was great excitement when a snake was found under the store tent.
The moral is to look carefully before-   (a) getting into bed,
                                          (b) putting your clothes on in morning,
                                          (c) eating your food.

August 3rd.   Scout Jamboree at Mount Edgcumbe. Lewis put on a clean pair of trousers having fallen into the fire. The Chief Scout, Lord Baden-Powell, arrived looking very young for his years. Poor Buster Bull was too small to see him go up the lane but we all got a good view as we marched past. Our Union Jack was carried by the British Contingent. Hurrah! Culmstock Scouters were in evidence as they kept the corner of the arena for the Trek Cart Race. One of the boys slipped and the wheel went over him, and his lanyard caught in the cart and round his foot dragging him along right in front of our A.S.M. One of the lady Scouters said "It would happen in front of poor old Stephen". After the Rally we went to the pictures and had supper at Lyons.

Hemyock Leisure Centre

An unusual start

In the 60's there was a Playgroup in the Village Hall run by Barbara Bowden, Barbara Churchill, Terry Doble's wife and Mrs. Clare. In order to raise funds, they decided to have an Art exhibition in the village to show things people had produced or things they had in their homes. Sam Lutley made all the hooks for hanging the exhibits. Polly and John Eden agreed to hold the show at Bean Close. The Head of the School, Mr. Clive Richardson,was keen that this should happen and the school children went to see it during the day and their parents went in the evenings. The Parents then made it clear to Mr. Richardson that they would like to know how to 'do' art and learn about it generally. So, in 1971 Hemyock Leisure Centre was started under the Chairmanship of John Eden. It met in the Primary School. No charge was made for the premises, just cleaning had to be paid for. It ran on four evenings a week with a cup of coffee and a chat halfway through the evening.

The groups were:-

Art: Maureen Diplock led the group. We had several exhibitions.

Local History: This got off the ground slowly until Professor Eurof Walters from Exeter came up to take it. Martin Dear was the Treasurer and the other committee members were Joan Gregory, Christine Meads and Mrs. Lipscombe from Bishopswood.

Music: It began with Mrs. Lipscombe singing to a guitar. Then Mr. Bobby Lane from Pipe's Cottage, a retired Army man, led the group which listened to records.

Play Reading Group: This was held at Rokeby because Christine Meads had to be around to answer the phone when her husband, Dr Meads, was on call! One of their events was to put on a shadow puppet show. Muriel Bater and Zita Lapworth were among the members.

Singing: Mr. Richardson was very keen to get this going. A meeting was called and the group sang in four part harmony, songs such as 'My love is like a red, red rose' and 'Go down Moses'. Eventually things got more ambitious and concert versions of Iolanthe and then The Gondoliers were put on. The women wore black skirts and pastel tops, and the men, dark trousers, white shirts and dark ties. 'H.M.S. Pinafore' was to be the first full performance; people such as Mrs. Elsie Board, Mrs. Jack Lutley and Mrs. Doris Farrant took part. Later, in collaboration with the school, 'Oliver' was performed. Eventually the Village Hall was thought to need an extension and £100 was needed. The PTA put up half and the Leisure Centre agreed that they would pay for the other half. Performances are still put on there.

After several years the new school was built and the other Leisure Club activities were dying off so it was decided to wind up the Centre. Instead of donations to charity, which had been the usual thing, the remaining funds were given to the school for books and to the Cystic Fibrosis Trust. It became clear that the Music Group was the greatest strength so it remained as a separate activity. So out of the ashes of the Leisure Centre emerged the Hemyock Singers, still active today with their musical show in the Autumn and Sacred Music at Easter.

Dances

Dances were held in the school, with music provided by a piano or accordion and sometimes, when dance band music was first heard on the radio, the men would rig up the radios with wires all over the place. Concerts were also held using local talent. Mrs Pike remembers her aunt singing, 'A Gypsy's Warning'. Printed sheets of the songs were handed out to the audience.

Bell Ringing in Culmstock

Harry Perry was the Sexton so when someone died he tolled the bell, one toll for every year of the deceased's life. Everyone in the village would come to their front doors and count the number of strikes and discuss with neighbours whose death it could be. It was particularly poignant when it only tolled once or twice.

Mr. Dennis Hoile began bell ringing in 1949. They rang twice on Sundays, 11a.m. and 6p.m. and on Easter Morning at 6 o'clock to avoid Holy Communion at 7a.m. and 8a.m. They also rang for weddings and a half muffled peal for funerals. The ringers didn't go to the church service except on special occasions such as Harvest Festivals; then they would rush out at the end of the service and up into the bell tower to ring another peal. Each year the ringers went round the village collecting money for their annual outing, when they would visit three different churches and ring the changes in each.

When Langdon Hine first started ringing, his arm got tangled in the rope and he was carried upwards until his head hit the ceiling. Although badly shaken he continued bell ringing. Walt Milton collapsed when ringing one Sunday morning and lay unconscious in the belfry, the ambulance men had great difficulty in carrying him down the winding narrow steps, and he died in hospital a few days later.

Keep Fit

Mary came to live at Clayhidon in the late 1960's, and we soon discovered that she had taken Keep Fit Classes before moving to Devon. The word soon spread and before long there were enough people interested to make a start at keeping fit.

Clayhidon Village Hall was booked and Bill played the piano by ear for our exercises. Mary soon had us moving in time to the music. Bill was brilliant, he seemed to know every tune that had ever been written, and if by chance there wasn't a tune to fit the rhythm of one of Mary's exercises within seconds Bill would have composed one. It was wonderful doing Mary's exercises to Bill's music, I would arrive home at the end of the evening singing happily and feeling I could climb mountains! I must admit that next morning was sometimes a different story with aches, pains and stiffness in places I didn't know existed.

As time went on the class grew and moved to Hemyock and also to Smeatharpe, and we went to various places giving exhibitions. The class is still going strong, with Mary and Madge still leading the exercises, and Bill still at the piano. Some of the original members are still there, and it looks as if it will go on for ever.

Gardeners' Question Time

After the 1939-45 war, food was still very scarce so a Garden Society was formed in Culmstock so one got seeds much cheaper. As time went on, it was decided to hold one of the gardeners' quizzes with the locals, and a man came up from Exeter to be quiz-master. One of the gardeners had to answer this question "What reptiles do we find in the garden?" "Bloody cats, dogs, rabbits, fowls and pigeons" came the reply. "Ah", he said, "I see you know your onions".

Eventually the Gardening Club faded away, so that was the end of cheap seeds when 10/- would have bought enough for the season. Hemyock Gardeners' Association was started in 1952 and seeds can still be bought at low prices.

Whist

Dora's father, Vic Bale, used to go to Whist Drives at Christmas, and one night he won a goose. He went home on his bike with it on his carrier. At one o'clock in the morning, he plucked the goose all the way up over the hill and left the feathers all over the road and up to Chester Lowman's front door. Another night Dora's father came home one night, and we were sound asleep in the bedroom. The door opened, and we wondered what the devil it was. He threw a brace of rabbits on the floor, which he had won at the Whist Drive.

Shooting the Ferret!!

In the early 1930's my father used to invite my mother's two brothers down from Bristol to a shooting party. On one occasion a member shot too quickly at the burrow and they shot the ferret! They were surprised and relieved next year to find that the ferret survived, though blind in one eye, and was still working.

Local Entertainment

I remember the annual visits to Bristol pantomime by charabanc. One year, shortly after leaving the village, a glass and bottles of home-made wine were passed round the coach so a lot of people didn't enjoy the pantomime that evening!
– there was a late bus on Saturday night from Taunton at 10.30 p.m. and in the snow the buses struggled to Culmhead or only as far as the White Lion.
– there was the mobile cinema in the Village Hall, I recall such films as 'The Cruel Sea', 'The Blue Lamp' and Dickens' 'Great Expectations' with the poor jilted Miss Haversham in her rotting wedding dress and mice eating the cake!
– a concert party called the 'Flutterbies' used to come from Exeter but when their jokes became slightly near the mark their visits ceased.

The Half Moon Inn

This was my second home for 25 years - it is a fascinating building. I heard that the top room, now the skittle alley, was originally used as a resting station for pilgrims going to Dunkeswell Abbey. The Inn has the unusual feature of an entrance to Clayhidon Church. Whenever there was a social event of any kind requiring water for teas and refreshment, the locals would not use water from the pub, thinking it drained from the graveyard at the rear in which some cholera victims were buried. So, on the morning of any event a farmer would supply the water from his own source in large milk churns.

The customers were almost exclusively local, mostly cider drinkers and practically all had their own drinking vessels. In the bar there was a round cast iron stove to supply heat to the premises. The beer and cider were kept, as was usual in those days, on a gantry at the back of the bar. The place was very spartan but had a tremendously friendly atmosphere. When I had been established as a 'regular' I was asked by the landlord if I could organise Saturday night dances as I was then the Entertainments Officer for the Wellington branch of the R.A.F. Association. They became popular and eventually proved a great success. The dances were held in the top room and I varied them a little by introducing 'Special' nights, Fancy Dress, Tarts and Vicars, etc. I also organised a run from the Half Moon to the Merry Harriers and a return match from the Merry Harriers to the Half Moon. In the early post war years the Half Moon had no mains electricity so power was generated by a Petter engine in a room in the outside toilet. The view from the back of this toilet across the valley is gorgeous and the lane at the other side of the valley was always known to the locals as 'Red Lane' on account of some ancient battle being fought on the site.

A friend of mine, Nellie Lentle, and I both worked in Gentlemen's service when we were young. Nellie worked at Craddock House for the New Family, and I worked at Leigh Court for Admiral Parker. We both had Thursday afternoon off duty and always spent it together. One hot summer afternoon we went up the river to bathe. One of us had left our clothes quite near the river's edge.

All of a sudden the water came rushing down and swept one lot of clothes down river. So as to look respectable going home we divided up the dry set of clothes, I can't remember who had what. We did hear later that a fender had been pulled out of the river and sent a rush of water down. We were not to know whether this was true or not. All I know is, we both had a shock.

❖ ❖ ❖

May

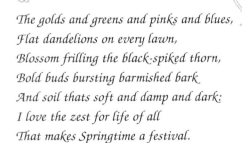

I love this Springtime festival,
The lust and thrust and zest of all
The tall and tender juice-plump weeds
Leaping bursting from their seeds,
Leaf-lights gleaming in the trees,
Gold-flecked fields and buzzing bees,
Lush crushed grass sap on my shoes,

The golds and greens and pinks and blues,
Flat dandelions on every lawn,
Blossom frilling the black-spiked thorn,
Bold buds bursting barnished bark
And soil thats soft and damp and dark:
I love the zest for life of all
That makes Springtime a festival.

Wheels

My father came to live in Hemyock in 1911 to Rose cottage next to the Baptist Chapel and school. He married and had two girls and a boy before I came on the scene on my mother's fortieth birthday. When I was old enough I only had to cross the road to go to school. I enjoyed school life particularly gardening on the edge of the playing fields. Every boy had a plot of ground to look after where we grew vegetables. My father was a keen gardener and I followed in his footsteps from a very early age. Mr Prowse, the headmaster, saw how well kept our garden was next door so he soon had me tending his garden. Before the war we had Christmas parties but one year a boy was caught misbehaving. He picked up a shovel and chased Mr Prowse around the class. He was a bit of a terror and was always into mischief. The Christmas party was cancelled after that so we all had to suffer because of one boy.

I had a mini motor on my bike which worked off the back wheel. One day I was pedalling along the road towards Culmhead on a Sunday afternoon and a police car pulled up and stopped me. He couldn't understand why I was cycling so fast. He had been intrigued by this so he had recorded the speed and I was doing 30 m.p.h.!

A local butcher used to go round the farms and buy a pig or two during the war. Food was rationed and the local policeman was on duty one day when the butcher came down in his van. He drove straight down to the shop without stopping and took out the pig and hung it in the window. The next day the meat inspectors came out as the policeman had reported the incident. They went straight to the refrigeration room but found no pig. They didn't think of looking in the window! I was in the Scouts and Mr Thorn, our Scout master, cycled all the way up the steep hill from Wellington. One day we went up to Culmhead and saw the Czechs and Poles in the camp having a boil up of slugs and snails. We didn't fancy any!

When I was fourteen I left school and went to work for Stanley Doble mending bicycles and motor bikes. New motor bikes were put on the train in Birmingham and arrived the next day in Hemyock.

Mr Thorn was a music teacher and played the hand pumped organ in church. He taught me to play piano accordion and the violin and soon I wanted my own Hohner instrument from Germany. It came and cost me £12.

❖ ❖ ❖

After the war on a visit to Lyme Regis I bought an ice cream. It tasted terrible, just like water and no sugar, but it was ice cream and I ate it all.

Highways and Byways

In the early nineteen hundreds, Culmstock Rural District Council (Clayhidon, Hemyock, Culmstock, Burlescombe and Holcombe Rogus) was responsible for road maintenance in each area. By-roads were still stone - surfaced before the general use of tar macadam.

Flintstones

Councils would ask for tenders to supply cracked flint stones measured by the cubic yard. These stones were dug by hand from local hill areas. They were then hauled by horses in carts specially made for the purpose to sidings by the road. The stone-cracker, wearing wire-gauze goggles and wielding a stone hammer, would sit by the pile of stones. He would crack them to a size which would go through a two and a half inch riddle. All flints have a grain and an experienced stone-cracker would know where to strike in order to crack them with a minimum of effort. The cracked stones would be stacked in a long continuous line, about two yards wide at the base, approximately four feet high, tapering to a flat top two feet across. In Hemyock Parish, Jack Lilley dug stones at Burrow Hill Common, and Bill Moore was a skilled stone-cracker. Sidings were to be found at Byes, Culmbridge Road and Whitehall, among other places. Later the stones would be hauled to any roads in need of repair and spread evenly over the surface. Quarry waste would be shovelled over the surface area, which was well watered with a sprinkler on the back of a horse drawn water cart. Steamrollers, known as Puffing Billies, were used to level and compact the repaired road surface. A man called Jack Goldsworthy

had a cart and spent a lot of time carting stones from Thornbury Quarry down to the station to be loaded into trucks and taken away to build roads.

A Variety of Transport

From early days I recall riding in a pony and trap with yellow wheels. The first family car was a Standard 8, and on one occasion my brothers managed to drive it into a ditch from which it had to be pulled out by our horse, Punch. As a girl I cycled everywhere, often on my own, without any worry. We enjoyed a lot of freedom and in spite of the war it seemed a smaller and safer world than it is now.

Bearded Dr. Speffigew, who lived in South Street, visited Ford street on his horse. Mr Fitt, the School Inspector, called on his bike, puffing and blowing with his tummy resting on the bar as he walked up the Naps wearing breeches and leggings.

Steam wagons fed by coal, with solid rubber tyres, chugged up the road to White Ball Farm, and on Whit Tuesday, a coach, open to the weather, would take the chapel people to Sidmouth. I was too young to go, and cried when I saw my brother and sisters off on the trip of a lifetime.

Groceries were delivered from Mr. Jarman Baker's Stores, Wellington, once a fortnight, first on a bike, then motorbike, and finally a van.

My elder sister had a bicycle and rode to Langford Budville, being in service there. Carbide lamps were used and had to be pricked and cleaned, then filled with carbide and a little water which gave off a gas ignition.

Alan Cobham visited Chelston in his Tiger Moth aeroplane and Mum and Dad had a trip for about five minutes for 2/6. The following day the plane force landed at Gortnell just below us and a passenger broke a leg. It was a great experience to see the plane being dismantled.

The engine driver Percy and the fireman Ernie Pike used to drive the engine up to the bottom between Whitehall and Hemyock. They would get out and put wire traps all along the fence, then pick them up in the morning. They used to catch six or seven rabbits a night. A nice little side line! The milk train used to take about eleven tankers of milk out of the factory at 3p.m. to catch the train to London. The milk powder went later, or sometimes it would be taken in the morning.

Through the bad winter of 1963 my route was over Blagdon and the farmers brought their milk to the Lamb Inn. We had to use the main roads going down to Exeter and through Honiton and back. It was a long way but it was the only way home.

Sunday School Outing

When I was a kiddie, all the Sunday Schools here, Wesleyan, Baptist, and the Church used to have an outing to Teignmouth on the train every year. Sometimes coming home on the train out of 'Tivvy' Junction it struggled up the slope and then stopped for all the children to get out and push the train. It was able to move again with the weight of the children off the train.

The train journeys to the seaside became a village affair and the village was empty for a day. These outings were organised usually by the Sunday School and extra carriages were put on the train. Leaving Hemyock very early in the morning, we were in Exeter by 9 o'clock after changing trains at Tivvy Junction and from Exeter we travelled to Teignmouth. Once when my father was home on leave he took me and my brother out in a rowing boat. I was very frightened and did not enjoy it at all. Knitted swimsuits looked wonderful until they were wet, and then they took on a whole new shape!

Street Lighting

When I was about seven, my brother lit the oil lights. Every Friday afternoon we used to go round with a hand cart, with a tin of oil and we used to clean the lights, fill them up and then go round and light them when it got dark. At eleven or twelve at night they were turned off

The Last Train

The Culm Valley Railway was opened in 1876, and the last passenger train left Hemyock on 14th September 1963. I bought the last train ticket to Tiverton junction. As we approached each station it was quite exciting as detonators would explode on the line and people cheered. I would not have missed it for anything.

❖ ❖ ❖

One of Nature's Gentlemen

I was born in School Farm, Otterford on October 7th 1908. When my brother started school there was no school house, but one was built later by two men from Wellington. They lodged with my parents while building it and carted all the materials from Wellington by horse drawn wagons. Flint stone and sand were quarried locally. The house was completed in 1913 when I started school. My father kept a lot of pigs which caught swine fever. The inspectors came in their white coats and the pigs were buried in a field nearby. A pit was dug and covered in lime then the pigs were put in and more lime until the job was completed.

When we moved to Bolham Water in 1914 all the furniture was carted in horse drawn wagons. The Hebditch fowl houses were on wheels and were towed behind the wagons. My father still kept pigs and had help to kill, scald and dress the pigs before taking them to Hemyock station and on to Bristol to be sold.

My father used to go to Bampton Fair which was twenty or more miles away. He bought a colt along with many others and they all herded them together on the same road home, dropping out when they passed their houses. At Tiverton Junction there were only two left and as it was still a long way home they put them on the train and they were delivered to Hemyock station next morning.

In the winter of 1918 we had a very bad winter with a lot of snow. My brother Tom was a carter and only sixteen years old when he was sent with Fred Doble with two wagons and four horses to the far side of Uffculme to collect furniture for my aunt and uncle. It was snowing when they started so Mother filled a quart bottle with hot tea put in a stocking and wrapped in flannel to keep it warm as there was no thermos in those days. When they were late arriving home my father and I walked two or more miles to look for them by the light of the hurricane lantern. We eventually saw them coming slowly with the loaded wagons and the family of six riding on the top!

One wagon had to be abandoned before Ridgewood hill where they were allowed to park under a hanging roof. The remaining wagon had all four horses to pull them to Churchinford where that too was left for several days until the weather abated.

Every day my father took the milk to a collecting point where the milk was put on a wagon to be taken to the Hemyock factory. In the summer there was surplus milk which my mother delivered by pony and trap.

In 1919 we moved to another rented farm in Otterford when my brother and I helped in road maintenance. We were hired, with the horse and cart, to take cracked stones from the heaps to spread on the roads. They would be levelled along the road and sand was spread over the stones. I was engaged with a horse and cart to spray water over the sand to prevent it sticking to the roller. The steam roller would go over them a few times to get them flat and level. This completed the road building in those days.

I learned to drive when I was 17 in 1925 in a T Ford van belonging to the baker. His son let me drive on a stretch of unclassified road and that was my only lesson! I had a licence for all types of vehicles which I applied for with no test! I did pass a heavy goods test later in the war but continued to drive all types of vehicles from motor cycle, baker's van, butcher's van to lorries and cars without a test. I drove hired cars for weddings and funerals and even an ambulance. Quite a change from driving the horse and wagon. I gave up driving when I was over 88 so had 70 years in the driving seat!

High Days and Holidays

A Boy's Eye View of Culmstock Fair

For we boys Culmstock Fair was the best day of the year. It was always on the Monday preceding the 24th May (we don't know why), and we had a day's holiday from school.

Some time before we would wander around the lanes looking for a nut or ash stick, it had to be long and straight with a fork at the top. We would cut it out and take it home and whittle away with a pocket knife peeling off bands of bark to make a stripy pattern; this was our 'Fair Stick' to use on fair day to help herd the cattle, hooking our thumb in the fork, feeling very grown up.

On the Sunday our mothers would roast a huge joint in the oven to be ready for the aunts, uncles, relations and friends who came the next day to enjoy the excitement and do business at the fair. Hurdles were erected in the field at the top of the hill (on the Uffculme road) ready to pen the sheep. One old drover would arrive and sleep overnight in Hoopalongs Linhay ready to start work early next morning.

We always woke early on Fair day as there was lots to do and, if we were lucky, pennies to earn. Windows of houses abutting the road were boarded up and gardens were barricaded. Stalls were set up outside the Ilminster Inn and National School, sugared almonds, fairings and toffee apples were set out. Mr. Phillips, who traded as The Farmers Friend, had a stall loaded with pocket knives, rope, boots, caps, trousers, pots and pans, etc.

Soon farmers and drovers would be herding their store cattle into the village, having walked many miles after an early morning start. This was when we could join in and help by keeping them in their lots and not letting them get muddled up or stray. There would be animals filling the road from the Strand, The Cleeve, Fore Street, Silver Street and right up to Hillmoor, some were quite frightening with enormous horns and we would feel very brave with our fair sticks holding them back.

The sale ring was at the crossroads at the top of Town Hill and slowly the lots were driven along as their turn to be auctioned came. Then would come the time when we boys could slip up to the linhay in the sheep field, where we could get free bread and cheese given out by Mrs. Burrows (such cheese, the best we've ever tasted). Bert Hooper was giving out the cider, and we boys always managed to get some, in fact more than once we managed to get more than one glass in spite of a watchful eye being kept. Some of the drovers, after a very early start, a long walk and several glasses of cider would soon be taking a nap under the hedge! Then the cattle had to be driven down the village and over the bridge where cattle trucks were waiting at the railway siding and there were lorries lined up on the road. There was much swishing and we boys learnt some new swear words as the cattle were loaded up.

The pubs had been open all day which, looking back, must have added to the general air of excitement and jollity. The final entertainment for us was sitting on the churchyard wall opposite the Ilminster Inn watching the farmers and drovers emerge in various stages of joviality, some unsteady on their feet, some in a fighting mood, and some just plain happy and so were we.

Culmstock Flower Show

For several weeks my mother would be anxiously watching the way the black currants were ripening, and as usual the postman would find an excuse to call round the back of the house and find an excuse to look up the garden - he was hoping to show black currants as well. We all wore our best dresses, starched and ironed, and had our hair washed and rinsed in rainwater and then crimped with paper for Bank Holiday Monday, Flower Show Day. My mother would take her sweet peas and black currants down to be judged. Already swing boats, coconut shies and roundabouts were being set up in the field by the school. Heavy horses would be led through the village, their brasses gleamed and jingled in the sun and their coats shone from being brushed. They lined the road from Town Hill to Hillmoor, waiting to be judged.

At two o'clock the village band led the way from the Ilminster Inn to the show ground, and we children followed behind. First came the races:- hurdles, one mile (Len Nethercott always won that), children's races, pony races, greasy pole and the cart horse Derby (Mr. Wilfred Tucker always won that). There was always a lovely tea with chudleys and cream and then the cash prizes would be given. In the evening there would be a big crowd to watch the village band playing conducted by Mr. Shaddock outside the Railway Inn, the older girls would then go to the dance in the long room at the Ilminster Inn.

Peace Celebrations

My first recollection of a Special Occasion in Clayhidon was the Peace Celebrations after the 1914-1918 war. It was held in the summer of 1920. We were all sent to school in the morning with our best 'pinnies' on and brightly shone boots. No public holidays then! The photographer came and we all had our photos taken. I think there is still one in the History Group's archives.

Then we had our sandwich dinner early and all lined up to march to the Four Cross Way at the top of the hill. Once there we had a much needed rest under the shade of a tall beech hedge on the left, to await the arrival of the Wellington Town Band. We followed on behind the band over to the Church where there were all sorts of things going on in Garland's Bower. Various races had been organised for the school children after which we had a scrumptious tea in the marquee which had been erected.

Death of the King

I can remember the death of George V. I was out walking with my dog - and the delivery van from North Town Stores in Taunton stopped and the driver said "The King is dead!" I was shocked. I can remember the Abdication and felt Edward VIII would have made a good King. We knew so little of the background then, not like today with Charles, Diana and Camilla!

Coronation 1937

There were two great events in 1937: the Coronation of King George VI and Queen Elizabeth, and I came into the world. The only soap at hand for my very first wash was a block of lifebuoy carbolic, and the midwife said that would be fine. Could that be the reason why I am still wrinkle free?! Whatever happened to lifebuoy carbolic? To celebrate the birth of his grandson, my grandfather had a little too much alcohol, had an accident with his car and never drove again. I think we must have had friends in high places because I had a Coronation mug five months before I was born!

Culmstock Beacon

A Snippet from the Scout log:-
The Troop and pack went up on Wednesday, May 5th, to begin building the Beacon fire on Culmstock Beacon. Mr. McElwee and Mr. Knowlman gave us wood, and Mr. Bert Williams gave

❖

On the actual VE and VJ nights on 1945 bonfires were lit in the Churchinford village square. My aunt was so terrified that the petrol pumps would blow up that she came with water hose. She was not very popular!

❖

❖

Before the Coronation of Queen Elizabeth II Mr Cox put up the first TV aerials just in time for the event but he fell off the ladder and badly damaged his ankle.

❖

60 tyres and 5 gallons of sump oil. Mr. Squires of Purchase Farm very kindly gave the supporting poles and hauled wood and browse. On Tuesday evening it had been decided that the Court of Honour should guard the Beacon but as there was heavy rain they did not go up until 8 a.m., on Wednesday the 12th (Buster had to be hauled out of bed!) They used Mr. Thorne's ice cream barrow for most of the gear, whilst the bell tent went up on the A.S.M.'s sidecar.

The Camp was officially visited by the A.S.M. on Wednesday at 12a.m. and again on Thursday at 1p.m. He found everything satisfactory through he admitted there was room for improvement. But on the whole he was quite satisfied. (Unusual for him!) Mr. Jim Collier lit the fire at 10 p.m. and several kind friends gave money for rockets. As a result we managed to send off 43. They were such happy, carefree days, full of fun and games with no forebodings of the war that was to come and change all our lives.

Hemyock Carnival

For Hemyock's first Carnival in 1940, I was given the job of making the dresses for the Carnival Queen and her four Maids. The material was white cotton, trimmed with silver tinsel, using Christmas decorations! The Queen's crown was decorated with coloured beads and made by the Factory Manager's wife - she also made a cloak of red velvet. I wore my great grandma's crinoline dress which created a lot of interest. My mum made a poke bonnet and dad made me a parasol.

Coronation 1953

Mr Digby, a dentist, lived in Garlandhayes, and owned the only TV set so we all piled into the sitting room to watch the Coronation. Mr Digby had a generator as there was no electricity in Garlandhayes at that time!

It was a lovely morning and at mid day the village turned out. The folk dancing club met in the square and we did the Helston Furry Dance (floral dance) down in the Recreation Field. Miss Thelma Lowry and Mrs Evelyn Pike led the dancing and the rest followed. Music was played by Dennis Salter on the accordion, fun and games were had by all during the afternoon, with tea for everyone in the Parish Hall. Mary Savage and I delivered tea to all people who could not attend. It took all afternoon, Mary drove her car and I ran in and out of the houses in the pouring rain. The last call was a lady at Ashculme. She put the box on the floor and kicked it down the passage. Her daughter picked it up and said "Thank you very much, I am sure Mother will enjoy it" I hope she did!

In the evening a whist drive was held in the Church room and a Social in the Parish Hall. The Girl Guides did a pageant and a dance was held at the St Ivel factory.

Smeatharpe Carnival

Smeatharpe Carnival was the big event of the year. It was always held in October and we had a big bonfire. There was a torch light procession of horses and wagons, representing different items, mostly comic. One year a goat farmer paraded the goats which he kept on the moor. We made halters of red berried branches to go round their necks and they were led by a rope.

The Carnival procession was led by the Mayor and Mayoress. All the wagons were lit with torches on a long stick with a tin on the end to hold the paraffin rags. We topped up with paraffin as we went along. We had a brass band to dance to afterwards in the marquee. It was sometimes so muddy that we lost our shoes in the mud but we still enjoyed ourselves. Everybody used to dance and we needed to dance to keep warm, because it was always cold at that time of the year. The marquee was always full

of people enjoying the refreshments and home made ginger wine. People came from far afield - Ottery St Mary did a tableau. There was an annual auction behind the pub where bullocks and farm implements were sold. The Carnival raised hundreds of pounds for the hospital in Honiton.

Thinking Day

The nearest Sunday to Thinking Day, February 22nd, we had a Church Parade. I carried the Union Jack and Mary Woodgate carried the Guide Flag. We were all right going up to the altar but coming out I slightly touched the chandelier, which made it swing a bit. I was looking for the step thinking that I might trip up, but worse was to come; Mary managed to get her flag caught up in some wire netting which was in the ceiling of the porch, and had to have help to move it. The new flags had been dedicated that day so Miss Lowry was far from pleased. I often sit in church and watch to see if anyone is going to hit the chandelier. It has happened once or twice.

Sunday School Treats

When we had our Sunday School treat in the field behind the chapel, the Stapley Sunday School joined us. The children and their mothers were brought in hay wagons drawn by horses. I'll never forget the joy of our Sunday School Treats. To wake up in the morning and remember that it was the day was so exciting. After the games, the school bell would ring for us to come in for tea. And what a tea!! Gorgeous chudleys with cream and raspberry or apricot jam, plus lots of cakes. My mother said that on one occasion a little boy was crying and when asked why by the Sunday School teacher he said it was because he could not eat anymore. The teacher said "Put some in your pockets" and he replied still crying "They're full!"

After more games, Mr Puttle scattered sweets in the grass for us to scramble over. Today it would be considered unhygienic but no one was any the worse for it. We went to Church Sunday School in the afternoon and the Baptist Chapel in the evening. We always had school clothes for the weekdays and a best dress for Sundays when there was no sewing, knitting or playing games. The

Rev. Tertius Pool gave us a Christmas tea and prizes, and in the summer there would be a party at Jerwoods with swings, and the Culmstock Band would play with Mr Shaddock conducting.

Summer Holidays

I remember the train fare from London to Taunton was 25/-, with children half price. I stayed at Whitmoor farm owned by Mr and Mrs Symons, their son and his wife. Breakfast was always about 10a.m. after milking had finished. Gran would fry thick slices of fat bacon with fried potatoes left over from the day before. The breakfast always tasted good. It was cooked over an open fire using faggots of wood with kettles and saucepans hung on hooks over the fire.

At dinner there was plenty of rabbit and pork. The pork was home cured with salt and hung from the ceiling in the kitchen. For tea and supper there were thick slices of buttered bread, with home made jam. Sometimes we would have junket or rice pudding with cheese for the men.

I was never keen to visit the lavatory at the top of the garden. It was a bench type with two holes, and the toilet paper was newspaper cut into small squares and attached to the wall with string.

Granddad owned a bull. There was no artificial insemination so when any neighbour brought their cow along to the farm, my brothers and sister and I would be rushed in, all curtains drawn so that we could not see the cow and the bull together.

Gran always put on a clean white apron on Sunday afternoon and we would be taken for a walk around the fields. The postman delivered on his bicycle and

was always ready for a chat. He was never in a hurry.

I stayed in a cottage owned by Mr Lowman, the local blacksmith. The trains ran at the bottom of the garden and we would run down and wave to the driver just like the Railway Children in the film. Drinking water had to be fetched in stone pitchers from the pump opposite Whitehall Manor. When I was on holiday my aunt was never short of water as I was always keen to fetch some and visit Whitehall Halt to talk to the young porter. Five years later he became my husband. The front door of the cottage was open to everyone passing and they were expected to pass the time of day. Uncle was a blacksmith so there were always plenty of visitors.

While I was growing up, my parents used to bring us children to Hemyock every year for our annual summer holidays. The same village green, swings and Parish Hall stand today. As a young child I stayed with my Grandma and Granddad in their house in Eastlands, when my Granddad was still a village postman. He kept chickens down the road and I loved to go and feed them. In later years, my parents and younger sister would stay with my grandmother in her much smaller bungalow overlooking hills and fields farmed by other members of the family. We would sit outside in the sun shelling peas grown in the garden. Those were the days before the estates were built, when the roadside hedges were high and there were no street lights. We could walk around the hills safely, with a packed lunch, with no lorries driving through the village.

At the height of the hay making time we would have a big family reunion, sitting on the hay bales on my uncle's farm on Dunkeswell aerodrome enjoying our picnic with fun and games under the watchful eye of all the great aunts. Afterwards we would enjoy a cup of tea in the old farm house. This had stone flags on the floor and no electricity, and we would sit on benches right inside the fire place.

When I got married my husband and I went overseas to the Middle East, on Mission work. We would come home every two years or so and bring our children to Hemyock to see their Grandma and Granddad (my parents) and to meet cousins and relatives. One day back in Egypt, my young daughter was asked by her primary school teacher "Where is the centre of the world?" Unhesitatingly my daughter replied "Hemyock!"

Save the Hungry Fund

One very wet winter's night in 1967 when only a few people had gone to a Lenten meeting, the Rector drew their attention to the fact that there was a very bad famine in Bihar, India. This was the first time that a famine on this scale had been reported in any depth on television and people were horrified by the things they saw and heard. So began the Culm Valley 'Save the Hungry Fund'. One of the members, Peter Reed, had the idea of asking St Ivel if dried milk powder could be bought for them to send out to India. St Ivel agreed!

The news spread throughout the Deanery. The Tiverton Weekly promoted the idea and money started to come in. £2,000 was raised in a short time. Local television heard about it and filmed a lorry leaving the milk factory in Hemyock with milk powder on board en route for India. At a service in the church two Hemyock choir boys took tins of milk powder to be blessed before the tins started their journey. The Rev. Llewellyn-Jones went further afield, the Deanery and Culm Valley were deemed to be too small, so Devon was to be targeted. This brought TV on the scene in the shape of Angela Rippon who interviewed Rev. Llewellyn-Jones. He brought examples of the amount of food eaten in one week by a Devon child and compared it with that eaten by an Indian child.

The organisers of the Devon County Show then offered a small marquee free of charge so that the word could be spread and more money collected. In 1996, by coincidence, Miss World was Miss India and she agreed to come to the County Show in Exeter.

The Rector was to look after Miss India while she was in the marquee where she would sign autographs in return for a donation! The Rector's wife said that she had never seen her husband take so much care over his appearance and was totally amazed to see her husband literally at Miss India's feet, cleaning her muddy shoes.

In total £17,000 was raised throughout Devon and the milk powder reached India safely. Letters came from numerous organisations who had benefited from the milk and it was stressed that the gift was a very real life saver because there would otherwise have been no milk in the area for the young children for about six months. One Head teacher of a school came to England on leave and brought photographs of her pupils receiving the milk.

❖ ✦ ❖

Back Home to the Blackdowns

My first visit to Malaysia was in 1956 when I went out by sea with our three small children to join my husband, Bryan. He was a soldier involved with the RAF in dropping supplies of medicine, food and mail to soldiers fighting the Communists in the jungle. He was a regular soldier and had just completed sixteen months service in Korea and Japan. Sadly, six weeks after we joined him, he was killed in a plane crash in the dense jungle in Tapah Hills. Three New Zealand air crew, two British soldiers and two civilian newspaper employees lost their lives in the crash. Miraculously, one soldier survived and was found in the jungle a week later. All those who had died were buried in the jungle and a year later they were moved to a military annexe of the Christian Cemetery in Kuala Lumpur. A memorial service was held before the children and I flew home to the Blackdowns.

At the time and for many years afterwards the fact that I played no part in the choice of flowers, hymns and service did not worry me, I was too busy bringing up the children. Then in 1990, I met many other war widows, two of them are now friends who keep in touch regularly. Our circumstances are so similar and comradeship grows, much like it did for our Servicemen husbands. We talked freely about our feelings, wondered how we would feel when we saw our husbands graves, for me the first time. But we were not prepared for the depth and range of our emotions.

After a very moving service of Remembrance at the cemetery, on the eleventh hour of the eleventh day of the eleventh month, we were invited to Kuala Lumpur Cathedral for lunch. Young people of the Cathedral entertained us with carols, and we were shown around the Cathedral and taken on a sight seeing tour. Their kindness and gratitude was overwhelming that our husbands had died defending their country against the Communists. I was fortunate enough to sit next to Ernie, a man whose ancestors had emigrated from Ceylon. We have kept in touch and he visits Bryan's grave and the graves of the husbands of my two friends and sends photographs of the flowers he puts on the graves and the crosses and wreaths he makes with red poppies. He is now 78 and certainly carries out practical Christianity which he believes in.

In 1994 I went to Malaysia with the British Legion after meeting up with my friends in Heathrow. We visited other cemeteries all beautifully cared for, and I met Ernie again with his wife Olga and son Rohan. This cemented our friendship still further. On this trip we were joined by Charlie Chester and a Radio 2 crew recording a programme on Malaysia. As a result I was heard on Charlie's programme and was later asked to take part in a programme on bereavement on West Country Live. I also had a letter from one of the SAS men who had found the bodies after the crash in the jungle.

Losing Bryan so early in our married life was devastating, but life goes on and I have travelled to places, met people and made friends, all of whom have enriched my life. But when the children and I flew home in 1956 to live with my parents in Culm Davy it was great to be among friends and family and to live in a village in the Blackdowns, like Hemyock, so caring and supportive.

A Last Thought

Gone are the old-time smithies and the great farm horses. The little village shops have vanished. The wells are buried. Pipes with chlorinated water have taken their place. So everything has changed for good or bad? They call it progress.

It is good and comforting to remember that since the world began, the sun has risen and set, the moon has shed her quiet light, the stars have shone and twinkled. So we are given some understanding of a stabilising force and an Eternity in which an Everlasting God reigns.

Contributors

We are grateful to the following people who have made generous contributions to this book by sharing their memories with us. We apologise if we have omitted anyone by mistake.

Pam Adams	Doreen Cutler	Dennis Kerslake	Ern Robjohn
Bill Alford	Pamela Dowson	Vera Kerslake	Nora Robjohn
Bill Andrews	Evelyn Doble	John Knowlman	Audrey Salter
Jackie Ascott	Chris Drake	Wladic Kunda	Ken Salter
Bill Bartlett	Pat Earland	Ruby Laidlaw	Les Sandford
Sylvia Bates	Polly Eden	Fred Lawrence	Hilda Sanders
Betty Blackmore	John Eden	Joan Lawrence	Mercy Seaford
Frank Board	Jack Edwards	Fleur Layzell	Art Shire
Barbara Bowden	Margaret Fisher	Blanche Loosemore	Betty Shire
Bill Bull	Harold Fisher	Phyllis Lowman	Nita Slowman
Ralph Buttle	Shirley Gregory	Norman Lowman	Robin Stallard
Gladys Channon	John Griffin	Skip Lowman	Betty Strawbridge
Ern Channon	Eve Grosse	Mollie Lutley	Betty Symons
Joan Churchill	Denis Hart	Eileen Marks	Stan Symons
Irene Clark	Dennis Hoile	Christine Matthews	Eddie Tartaglia
Lunch Club, Clayhidon	Barbara Hole	Daisy Middleton	Ruth Tartaglia
Gwen Coles	Ken Hole	Chris Moore	David Taverner
Jack Collard	Fay Hortop	Daisy Payne	Jane Ward
Stella Coombes	Nora James	Millicent Perkins	Bernard Wass
Fred Coombes	Joan Llewellyn-Jones	Evelyn Pike	Dulcie Webber
Joan Cooper	Margaret Kallaway	Chris Poole	Dennis Whitcombe
Dorothy Culverwell	Mary Kallaway	Vera Redwood	Bessie Woollacott